D0859894

THE LITTLE RED BOOK OF

LEADERSHIP LESSONS

THE LITTLE RED BOOK OF
LEADERSHIP LESSONS

Donald J. Palmisano

Foreword By
Governor Bobby Jindal

Skyhorse Publishing

Copyright © 2012 by Donald J. Palmisano

All Rights Reserved. No part of this book may be reproduced in any manner without the express written consent of the publisher, except in the case of brief excerpts in critical reviews or articles. All inquiries should be addressed to Skyhorse Publishing, 307 West 36th Street, 11th Floor, New York, NY 10018.

Skyhorse Publishing books may be purchased in bulk at special discounts for sales promotion, corporate gifts, fund-raising, or educational purposes. Special editions can also be created to specifications. For details, contact the Special Sales Department, Skyhorse Publishing, 307 West 36th Street, 11th Floor, New York, NY 10018 or info@sky-horsepublishing.com.

Skyhorse® and Skyhorse Publishing® are registered trademarks of Sky-horse Publishing, Inc. ®, a Delaware corporation.

www.skyhorsepublishing.com

10 9 8 7 6 5 4 3 2 1

Library of Congress Cataloging-in-Publication Data is available on file.

ISBN: 978-1-62087-191-1

Printed in China

Donald Palmisano has updates about his leadership books at www.onleadership.us

You can find his blog on leadership and health system reform at www.DJPupdate.com

He tweets at @DJPNEWS

DEDICATION

To Mary Ellen, Donna Ann, and Donald Jr., three wonderful children who taught me much about love and life. And may the grandchildren enjoy these quotes and leadership lessons as much as I enjoy their company. The future is theirs.

Contents

Contents

Foreword

Once again, Donald Palmisano brings insight and wisdom from proven and respected leaders to provide a handy compendium of advice for the leaders of today and tomorrow.

This collection puts forth perspectives on leadership when leadership is tested and matters most—in times of great adversity, mounting challenges, and real risk. In Louisiana, we've become all too aware of times like these in recent years.

From hurricanes to oil spills to a national economic recession, Louisiana has recognized and taken bold action by confronting our trials and tribulations with a passion to overcome. It is that fighting spirit that empowers leaders in our communities, companies, schools, and at every level of government.

The views presented in this book exemplify Donald's own accomplishments as a surgeon, businessman, author, and leader. Through his previous work, Donald has challenged all of us to figure out how to be better leaders. This new book is no exception, and I hope you are able to learn and grow from the vision Donald has presented in this book.

Governor Bobby Jindal
State of Louisiana

Introduction

Again and again, an enlightened and strong-willed individual has
pushed against the prevailing trends and the prevailing wisdom
to perform an act of courage that changed history.
—PAUL JOHNSON, "NEEDED: LEADERS OF COURAGE"
FORBES, MAY 7, 2007

• • •

This is a book of ideas; ideas devoted to leadership that promotes liberty.

This little red book continues the tradition of *On Leadership* and the expanded 2ⁿᵈ edition by further defining what it means to be a leader. In this book, I take a look back at chapters from my previous books and break down the essentials of leadership in illustrative quotes and a brief summary section at the end, called Lessons Learned. The book is divided into manageable sections that allow all the characteristics of leadership to be right at your fingertips. The dramatic stories of leaders found in the *On Leadership* editions are not in this work but are easily accessible in the original books.

Note the recurrent themes for leaders throughout the centuries as you read this book: homework, courage, decisiveness, action, persistence, and integrity.

Introduction

Use this book for inspiration when times are tough and you need encouragement to enter the arena of leadership. Few would dispute that leadership is desperately needed, now more than ever, to maintain America as a land of liberty and a beacon of freedom to the rest of the world. A return to individual responsibility, fiscal responsibility, and rejection of coercion are the building blocks of future greatness and exceptionalism. Vote for those who manifest these qualities. And for those who live in lands under repressive government and daily intimidation, a major purpose will be achieved if this book moves you closer to freedom.

Remember my message in the epilogue of *On Leadership*: Without the ability to identify true leaders the future is bleak. Disasters, wars, terrorism, and epidemics are just some of the challenges facing the world in the twenty-first century. Heroes and leaders are everywhere. It's our duty to recognize them. This is the price of freedom. Freedom is not free. Many died so we could be free. Let us not dishonor them.

Thanks to Tony Lyons, President of Skyhorse Publishing, for his continued encouragement, and to Skyhorse's Kristin Kulsavage, who artfully guided the manuscript and images through the labyrinth of the publishing process. And a special thanks to Robin, my wife, who gives loving support to my endeavors and is the best organizer of writing and all things important.

—Donald J. Palmisano,
April 2012

Pediatric office in New Orleans after Hurricane Katrina flooded it with 10 feet of water. The black mold is evident.

1

The Antithesis of Leadership

Be willing to make decisions. That's the most important quality in a good leader. Don't fall victim to what I call the "ready-aim-aim-aim-aim syndrome." You must be willing to fire.
—GENERAL GEORGE S. PATTON, JR.

• • •

Those who cannot remember the past are condemned to repeat it.
—GEORGE SANTAYANA, *REASON IN COMMON SENSE*

• • •

Zahn: "Sir, you aren't telling me you just learned that the folks at the convention center didn't have food and water until today, are you? You had no idea they are completely cut off?"

Brown: "Paula, the federal government did not even know about the convention center people until today."
—CNN'S PAULA ZAHN INTERVIEWING MICHAEL D. BROWN, DIRECTOR OF THE FEDERAL EMERGENCY MANAGEMENT AGENCY (FEMA), ON THE FOURTH DAY AFTER HURRICANE KATRINA STRUCK; *ON LEADERSHIP*

• • •

New Orleans morgue flooded during Hurricane Katrina and temporary morgue setup in St. Gabriel, Louisiana. Here Donald J. Palmisano does a tour with Coroner Dr. Frank Minyard to view forensic identification site full of experts trying to identify bodies with DNA samples and other tests. Death toll in New Orleans from Katrina highly influenced by failure to utilize lessons learned, including evacuation. Actions have consequences. Over fourteen hundred deaths occurred in New Orleans area as a result of Katrina; final number never determined.

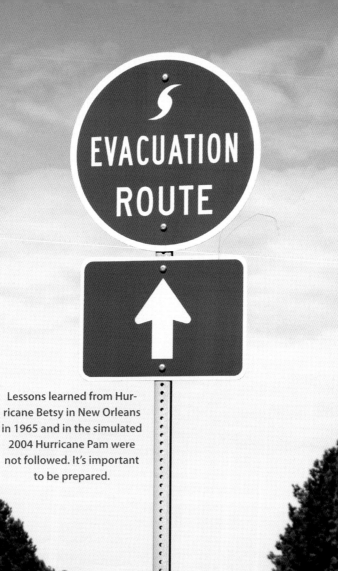

EVACUATION
ROUTE

Lessons learned from Hurricane Betsy in New Orleans in 1965 and in the simulated 2004 Hurricane Pam were not followed. It's important to be prepared.

FEMA press release of July 23, 2004, had this to say about the hypothetical Hurricane Pam: "We made great progress this week in our preparedness efforts . . . " Yet a year later, no one in the corridors of power appeared to have heeded the report's distinct and repeated warnings. Chairman Tom Davis of the Congressional Select Bipartisan Committee to Investigate the Preparation for and Response to Hurricane Katrina said on December 15, 2005, at the Hearing on Preparedness and Response in Louisiana, "[Hurricane Exercise] Pam was so prescient. And yet Katrina highlighted many, many weaknesses that either were not anticipated by Pam, or were lessons learned but not heeded. That's probably the most painful thing about Katrina, and the tragic loss of life: the foreseeability of it all." The Select Committee identified failures at all levels of government that significantly undermined and detracted from the heroic efforts of first responders, private individuals and organizations, faith-based groups, and others. . . . The institutional and individual failures we have identified became all the more clear compared to the heroic efforts of those who acted decisively. Those who didn't flinch, who took matters into their own hands when bureaucratic inertia was causing death, injury, and suffering. Those whose exceptional initiative saved time and money and lives.
—*On Leadership*

• • •

5

Editorial comment about Louisiana Governor Blanco blaming President Bush after Hurricane Katrina. ©2007 Steve Kelley of the *Times-Picayune*. Reproduced with permission.

Forming committees without action is a waste of time. Lessons learned from Hurricane Katrina and simulated Hurricane Pam were available and not used. ©2006 Steve Kelley of the *Times-Picayune*. Reproduced with permission.

✯ Leadership is action, not position.
— DONALD H. MCGANNON

• • •

We had no leadership. Hurricane Katrina arrived with a hands off Republican president in the White House, a shell shocked Democratic Maw Maw in the state house, and an inept hip-hop mayor in New Orleans. It was the perfect political equation for a disaster.
—BROBSON LUTZ, MD, FORMER NEW ORLEANS HEALTH DIRECTOR AND ORGANIZER OF THE "FRENCH QUARTER HEALTH DEPARTMENT IN EXILE" DURING HURRICANE KATRINA

• • •

Harsh words on this boarded up Oriental rug store in New Orleans. Fears of lawlessness prevailed in the aftermath of Hurricane Katrina.

Our recovery didn't happen by accident. It happened because we did what we were hired to do: to lead and manage by results.
—MICHAEL BLOOMBERG, MAYOR OF NEW YORK CITY, SPEAKING ON THE RECOVERY OF NYC AFTER THE TERRORIST ATTACK OF SEPTEMBER 11, 2001, DURING A VISIT TO NEW ORLEANS.

• • •

The question "Who ought to be boss" is like asking "Who ought to be tenor in the quartet?" Obviously, the man who can sing tenor.
—HENRY FORD

• • •

Anyone can hold the helm when the sea is calm.
—PUBLILIUS SYRUS, A FREED SLAVE, WHO WROTE MAXIMS IN THE FIRST CENTURY BC

• • •

Lakeview home in New Orleans with evidence of what
happens when a metal levee collapses during Hurricane
Katrina and onrushing water hits home.

LESSONS LEARNED

- The flawed or insufficient responses to the devastation in New Orleans from Hurricane Katrina are a textbook example of a lack of leadership.

- Leadership is not indecision. It is not procrastination. It is not disorganization. It is not lack of preparation. Leaders are not missing in action. Leaders are visible and make decisions in emergencies with the information available.

- False leaders are everywhere during times of calm, and then are inept and indecisive in an emergency.

- To prevent future failures, past failures must be studied. Lessons learned must be implemented.

$$(t)\} = \int_0^\infty f(t)e^{-st}dt = \sum_{n=0}^\infty \int_{nT} f(t)e^{-st}dt = \sum_{n=0}^\infty \int_{nT}$$

$$\left.\frac{-nT}{dt}\right| = \sum_{n=0}^\infty \int_0^T f(\tau)e^{-s(\tau+}$$

$$\int^T f(\tau)e^{-st}d\tau \sum_{n=0}^\infty e^{-}$$

$$\frac{a}{T} + h(t) - \qquad +T \qquad + h(t) - \frac{a}{T}(t-T$$

$$y = g \times f$$

$$f_1 * g$$

$$) * g(t)\} = \int_0^\infty \left(\int_\tau F(t-\tau \right.$$

$$= \left| \begin{array}{c} s+b \\ z= \end{array} \right.$$

$$F(z) g(t)e^{-s(z+\tau)}$$

$$(t) \qquad dt$$

$$(t)\} \cdot \mathcal{L}\{g(t)\} =$$

Homework can be tedious, but it is essential for leadership.

2

Advice from the Past: The Foundation of Success

Danger invites rescue; the cry of distress is the summons to relief.
—JUDGE BENJAMIN CARDOZO, 1921

• • •

Do your homework, have courage, and don't give up. Do that
and very little in life is impossible.
—POLICEMAN DOMINIC J. PALMISANO'S ADVICE TO
HIS SON, DONALD PALMISANO (DJP), AFTER HIS SON
SAID HE WAS GOING TO QUIT MEDICAL SCHOOL.

• • •

Abraham Lincoln is a leader who is remembered for his incredible integrity.

If one advances confidently in the direction of his dreams, and endeavors to live the life which he has imagined, he will meet with a success unexpected in common hours.
—HENRY DAVID THOREAU, *WALDEN*

• • •

Your time is limited, so don't waste it living someone else's life. Don't be trapped by dogma—which is living with the results of other people's thinking. Don't let the noise of others' opinions drown out your own inner voice. And most important, have the courage to follow your heart and intuition. They somehow already know what you truly want to become. Everything else is secondary.
—STEVE JOBS, CO-FOUNDER APPLE COMPUTER; 2005 STANFORD COMMENCEMENT SPEECH

• • •

[The] dictionary is the only place that success comes before work. Hard work is the price we must pay for success. I think you can accomplish anything if you're willing to pay the price.
—VINCE LOMBARDI

• • •

Always bear in mind that your own resolution to succeed is more important than any other.
—ABRAHAM LINCOLN

• • •

This win did not occur by chance!

I don't know the key to success, but the key to failure is trying to please everybody.
—BILL COSBY

• • •

One secret of success in life is for a man to be ready for his opportunity when it comes.
—BENJAMIN DISRAELI

• • •

Number one, great ideas matter. Number two, find passion. And, number three, be tenacious, be irrepressible.
—STEVE BALLMER, CEO MICROSOFT, USC COMMENCEMENT ADDRESS, MAY 13, 2011

• • •

Success is that old ABC—ability, breaks, and courage.
—CHARLES LUCKMAN

• • •

It takes courage to
get to the top.

LESSONS LEARNED

- A crisis frequently can test one's courage.

- The commitment to "do your homework, have courage, and don't give up" is vital to anyone seeking success.

- This advice is also important to leadership, but success alone does not equal leadership.

Take a moment and reflect why these leaders are depicted on Mount Rushmore. For perspective of size, note the men atop President Teddy Roosevelt.

3

The Essentials of Leadership: Success Cornerstones and More

Unbounded courage and compassion join'd,
Tempering each other in the victor's mind,
Alternately proclaim him good and great,
And make the hero and the man complete.
—JOSEPH ADDISON, *CAMPAIGN*, 1704

• • •

The most dangerous leadership myth is that leaders are born—
that there is a genetic factor to leadership. This myth asserts that
people simply either have certain charismatic qualities or not.
That's nonsense; in fact, the opposite is true. Leaders are made
rather than born.
—WARREN G. BENNIS

The time is now near at hand which must probably determine, whether Americans are to be, Freemen, or Slaves; whether they are to have any property they can call their own; whether their Houses, and Farms, are to be pillaged and destroyed, and they consigned to a State of Wretchedness from which no human efforts will probably deliver them. The fate of unborn Millions will now depend, under God, on the Courage and Conduct of this army—Our cruel and unrelenting Enemy leaves us no choice but a brave resistance, or the most abject submission; this is all we can expect—We have therefore to resolve to conquer or die.
—GEORGE WASHINGTON, GENERAL ORDERS, JULY 2, 1776

• • •

The alternative domination of one faction over another, sharpened by the spirit of revenge, natural to party dissensions, which, in different ages and countries, has perpetrated the most horrid enormities, is itself a frightful despotism. But this leads, at length, to a more formal and permanent despotism. The disorders and miseries, which result, gradually incline the minds of men to seek security and repose in the absolute power of an individual; and sooner or later, the chief of some prevailing faction, more able or more fortunate than his competitors, turns this disposition to the purposes of his own elevation on the ruins of public liberty.
—PRESIDENT GEORGE WASHINGTON, FAREWELL ADDRESS, 1796

• • •

An engraving by W. Humphreys of
President George Washington,
the gold standard for leadership.

First in war, first in peace, and first in the hearts
of his countrymen.
—FROM EULOGY FOR GEORGE WASHINGTON BY
HENRY "LIGHT-HORSE HARRY" LEE

• • •

Indomitable courage and his refusal to give an inch saved his
company . . .
—MEDAL OF HONOR CITATION FOR AUDIE MURPHY

• • •

I had a split-second decision to make. Do I let the train run over
him and hear my daughters screaming and see the blood? Or do I
jump in? I dove in and pinned him down.
—WESLEY AUTREY, THE MAN WHO SAVED AN
UNCONSCIOUS MAN BY COVERING HIM BETWEEN
THE SUBWAY TRACKS IN MANHATTAN.

• • •

People get injured and some die in war. Make sure we know why we are going to war and honor those who put their lives in harm's way.

Leaders distinguish themselves and are the stimulus to move others to action.

An enduring expression for Army leadership has been BE–
KNOW–DO.
Leadership is the process of influencing people by providing pur-
pose, direction, and motivation while operating to accomplish
the mission and improving the organization.
Warrior Ethos
I am an American soldier . . .
I will always place the mission first.
I will never accept defeat.
I will never quit.
I will never leave a fallen comrade.
—U.S. ARMY LEADERSHIP HANDBOOK

• • •

Leadership is clearly seeing the morally right decision, pursuing
it with courage and vigor, and sharing that vision; then, asking
no more of others than of yourself.
—LEAH MCCORMACK, MD, PAST PRESIDENT OF THE
MEDICAL SOCIETY OF THE STATE OF NEW YORK

• • •

Philip Howard, New York attorney, author, and Chair of
Common Good. Photo courtesy of DJP.

I can honestly say that I was never affected by the question of the success of an undertaking. If I felt it was the right thing to do, I was for it regardless of the possible outcome.
—GOLDA MEIR, PRIME MINISTER OF ISRAEL

• • •

Leadership is a kind of alchemy, able to transform thick mud into a smooth road.
—PHILIP HOWARD, ATTORNEY AND CHAIR OF COMMON GOOD, 2012

• • •

Leadership is not manifested by coercion, even against the resented.
—MARGARET CHASE SMITH

• • •

Whether a man is burdencd by power or enjoys power; whether he is trapped by responsibility or made free by it; whether he is moved by other people and outer forces or moves them—this is of the essence of leadership.
—THEODORE H. WHITE, *THE MAKING OF THE PRESIDENT*, 1960

• • •

A leader is that person who inspires hope and illuminates solutions with principled practical opportunities. A believer. A doer. A dreamer.
—MARCY ZWELLING, MD, PAST PRESIDENT AND CHAIR, AMERICAN ACADEMY OF PRIVATE PHYSICIANS

• • •

But when all is summed up, a man never speaks of himself without losing thereby. His self-accusations are always believed; his self-praise disbelieved.
—MICHEL DE MONTAIGNE, *OF THE ART OF CONVERSING*, 1580

• • •

Leaders live by their rhetoric. Actions impress followers more than words. Nelson Mandela embodies this trait.

The key to being a good leader is to focus on the mission and know
how to implement a plan without getting lost in the swamp!
Honey Island Swamp ©1985 Donald J. Palmisano.

Leadership starts with respecting others and paying attention to the needs of those around you. Smiling, shaking hands, touching and speaking to everyone that you see. Taking time to listen to what they say; respect them as people; helping them with small things; open the door for someone behind you; genuinely ask how they are feeling; ask what you can do to help them today. Respecting those who you lead, may lead, follow or just touch with your mind and eyes. You don't lead because you want to lead; you lead because they want to follow.
—NORMAN MCSWAIN MD, FACS, PROFESSOR OF SURGERY AT TULANE UNIVERSITY AND TRAUMA DIRECTOR AT SPIRIT OF CHARITY TRAUMA CENTER, ILH. CONSIDERED BY DJP TO BE A HERO OF HURRICANE KATRINA.

• • •

Leadership requires knowing where you are and having a clear vision of your desired destination. Something called a "leadership conference," if held by a hospital or such institution, is likely to be a "follow the leader" (they're the leader) and get others to follow along also.
—JANE M. ORIENT, MD, EXECUTIVE DIRECTOR OF THE ASSOCIATION OF AMERICAN PHYSICIANS AND SURGEONS

• • •

Just like superheroes, leaders do not retreat from adversity but courageously advance toward their goal. Leaders who gain power have a great responsibility to use it wisely.

The word *leader* first appears in English in about 1300 as *ledere*, and it is anciently derived from the words for path, or road, or the course of a ship at sea. Sir Gordon Brunton defined leadership as the intelligent and sensitive use of power. Leaders are able to set compelling goals and get others to share and pursue those goals. The bond between leader and follower is one of trust, flowing in both directions.
—FLOYD D. LOOP, MD, HEART SURGEON AND CEO CLEVELAND CLINIC 1989-2004, *LEADERSHIP AND MEDICINE*

• • •

Leadership is leading from the front, saying what needs to be done, doing what needs to be done, inspiring your followers, and persuading your critics.
—RICHARD L. REECE, MD, OF MEDINNOVATION

• • •

The six essential leadership attributes: set high standards; live your standards and mentor those who follow; create and share a vision; make the hard choices when necessary; be visible and outfront; and instill hope in those who follow.
—JOHN DI FRANCES

• • •

✦ The manager asks how and when; the leader asks what and why.
—WARREN G. BENNIS

• • •

Leadership is an art that includes possessing a vision based on unwavering principles, and an ability to inspire and encourage others to be leaders.
—W. JEFF TERRY, MD, PRESIDENT MEDICAL ASSOCIATION OF THE STATE OF ALABAMA (MASA), APRIL 13, 2012

• • •

His watchword— "It's up to you"! —is the irreducible attitude of the leader, the person who assumes responsibility for the outcome in whatever situation he finds himself.
—C. SCOT HICKS AND DAVID V. HICKS IN *THE EMPEROR'S HANDBOOK MARCUS AURELIUS*, A NEW TRANSLATION OF THE *MEDITATIONS*

• • •

LESSONS LEARNED

- The cornerstones of success are homework, courage, and persistence, but leadership requires that and more: integrity, decisiveness, communication, and inspiration, to name only a few.

- A leader is defined as a fully informed and decisive person with integrity who advances courageously toward a goal, and is determined to overcome obstacles and setbacks along the way.

- Sometimes a crisis tests a leader's ability to decide without delay, and to act on that decision when action is called for.

The Reading Room at the New York Public Library,
where some of the research for this book was done.

The J.P. Morgan book library vault shows the value
he placed on certain books.

4

A Primer on "Homework"

A little learning is a dangerous thing; drink deep, or taste not the Pierian spring: there shallow draughts intoxicate the brain, and drinking largely sobers us again.
—ALEXANDER POPE, *AN ESSAY ON CRITICISM*, 1709

• • •

Dr. John Snow proved by observation and study of the geographic location of cholera patients that cholera was spread by water contaminated from sewers. However, the medical establishment of the day ridiculed him and instead said, that cholera was due to miasma from decomposing animals, and proclaimed: "Theory is more despotic than reason."
—ON LEADERSHIP

• • •

The most terrible outbreak of Cholera which ever occurred in this kingdom . . . There was no particular outbreak of Cholera in this part of London except among the persons who were in the habit of drinking the water of . . . the pump-well . . . the sewer, which passes a few feet from the well . . .
—DR. JOHN SNOW, THE FATHER OF EPIDEMIOLOGY

• • •

The importance of research has been discussed for centuries as noted in this quote from Sun Tzu: "Know the enemy and know yourself; in a hundred battles you will never be in peril."
—SUN TZU, *THE ART OF WAR*

• • •

Reflection on the methods of old gives perspective. Perhaps Civil War Medal of Honor winner, college professor Joshua Chamberlain, was aware of this quote when he turned the tide of battle at Gettysburg rushing down Little Round Top hill, leading his men, all with swords drawn:
"A swift and vigorous transition to attack – the flashing sword of vengeance—is the most brilliant point of the defensive."
—KARL VON CLAUSEWITZ, 1817

• • •

Periscope viewing is a critical part of homework on a submarine, and homework is essential for all leadership. DJP in American submarine during JCOC63 described in *On Leadership*.

Read and do your homework. Having the right knowledge can make a difference.

Extend . . . analytic interest to the dust-buried accounts of wars long past as well as those still reeking with the scent of battle to bring to light those fundamental principles, and their combinations and applications which, in the past, have been productive of success.
—DOUGLAS MACARTHUR, ARMY CHIEF OF STAFF, 1935

• • •

After two nights in the medical library you will know more than ninety percent of the people in the world on a given topic.
—OSCAR CREECH, MD, CHAIR, TULANE DEPARTMENT OF SURGERY, 1961, TO DJP

• • •

Chance favors the prepared mind.
—LOUIS PASTEUR

• • •

Preparation, I have often said, is rightly two-thirds of any
venture.
—AMELIA EARHART, AMERICAN AVIATOR AND
FIRST WOMAN TO FLY SOLO ACROSS THE ATLANTIC
OCEAN

• • •

Science! True daughter of Old Time thou art!
Who alterest all things with thy peering eyes.
Why preyest thou thus upon the poet's heart,
Vulture, whose wings are dull realities? . . .
—EDGAR ALLAN POE, "SONNET: TO SCIENCE"

• • •

All the elements emitting such radiation I have termed *radioac-
tive*, and the new property of matter revealed in this emission has
thus received the name *radioactivity*.
—MARIE CURIE, FROM HER ACCEPTANCE SPEECH
FOR HER SECOND NOBEL PRIZE, THIS TIME IN
CHEMISTRY. SHE IS THE ONLY WOMAN TO BE
HONORED TWICE, DECEMBER 11, 1911.

• • •

Amelia Earhart opened new frontiers for women in flight. She was the first woman to fly across the Atlantic solo.

After the announcement of the 1911 Nobel Prize to Marie Curie but before she received the prize, it was alleged Marie Curie, a widow, was having an affair with a married man. A member of the Nobel Committee sent her a letter: "If the Academy had believed the letters . . . it would not, in all probability, have given you the Prize." *It was suggested she not show up for the ceremony. Madame Curie responded,* "You suggest to me . . . that the Academy of Stockholm, if it had been forewarned, would probably have decided not to give me the Prize, unless I could publicly explain the attacks of which I have been the object. . . . I must therefore act according to my convictions. . . . The action that you advise would appear to be a grave error on my part. In fact the Prize has been awarded for discovery of Radium and Polonium. I believe that there is no connection between my scientific work and the facts of private life. . . . I cannot accept the idea in principle that the appreciation of the value of scientific work should be influenced by libel and slander concerning private life. I am convinced that this opinion is shared by many people." *She showed up and received the award.*
—QUOTATION FROM *MARIE CURIE* BY RACHEL A. KOESTLER-GRACK

• • •

Marie Curie as portrayed by Susan Marie Frontczak of Storys-
mith®. http://www.storysmith.org/manya with permission.

Trust must be earned, and a leader learns through time and experience which sources can be trusted for reliable information, allowing quicker action. A reliable source provides objective facts —no hyperbole, no embellishment.
—DJP, *ON LEADERSHIP*

• • •

LESSONS LEARNED

- Homework is a necessary preparation for success and leadership. Use a variety of sources (starting with the Internet) to do as much homework as possible.

- Observation and logical pursuit of the evidence lead to the truth.

- Innovators frequently are in the minority and have to fight to get the truth recognized.

- The pursuit of excellence and leadership can be a lonely path, but success is worth the potholes encountered en route.

President Obama looks through DJP's *On Leadership* January 16, 2012 at Browne Education Campus. Reproduced with permission Reuters/Jonathan Ernest.

Courage is essential for leadership!

5

Courage

Whereas, Sir, you know courage is reckoned the greatest of all
virtues; because, unless a man has that virtue, he has no security
for preserving any other.
—SAMUEL JOHNSON, QUOTED IN JAMES BOSWELL'S
LIFE OF JOHNSON, 1791

• • •

Friends, I shall ask you to be as quiet as possible. I don't know
if you understand that I have just been shot . . . I was going to
make a long speech, so I cannot make a very long speech, but I
will try my best.
—THEODORE ROOSEVELT, IMMEDIATELY AFTER
BEING SHOT IN THE CHEST BY AN ASSASSIN, 1912

• • •

Courage is the virtue that President John F. Kennedy most admired. He sought out those people who had demonstrated in some way, whether it was on the battlefield or a baseball diamond, in a speech or fighting for a cause, that they had courage, that they would stand up, that they could be counted on.

—ROBERT KENNEDY

• • •

It is not the critic who counts, not the man who points out how the strong man stumbled, or where the doer of deeds could have done better. The credit belongs to the man who is actually in the arena, whose face is marred by dust and sweat and blood, who strives valiantly, who errs and comes short again and again, who knows the great enthusiasms, the great devotions, and spends himself in a worthy cause, who at best knows achievement and who at worse if he fails at least fails while daring greatly, so that his place shall never be with those cold and timid souls who know neither victory nor defeat.

—THEODORE ROOSEVELT AT SORBONNE;
RECIPIENT OF THE MEDAL OF HONOR AND THE NOBEL PEACE PRIZE

• • •

A definition of courage, essential to leadership

In whatever area in life one may meet the challenges of courage, whatever may be the sacrifices he faces if he follows his con-science—the loss of his friends, his fortune, his contentment, even the esteem of his fellow men—each man must decide for himself the course he will follow. The stories of past courage can define that ingredient—they can teach, they can offer hope, they can provide inspiration. But they cannot provide courage itself. For this each man must look into his own soul.
—JOHN F. KENNEDY, *PROFILES IN COURAGE*

• • •

Great accomplishments frequently
entail great risks.

Courage

Courage frequently is needed for a leader who brings about a paradigm shift. When that occurs, everyone is at the starting line. Expertise in the discarded method is of no value. Resistance will be encountered.

—DJP

• • •

Friends and Fellow Citizens, I stand before you tonight under indictment for the alleged crime of having voted at the last presidential election, without having a lawful right to vote. It shall be my work this evening to prove to you that in thus voting, I not only committed no crime, but, instead, simply exercised my citizen's right, guaranteed to me and all United States citizens by the National Constitution, beyond the power of any State to deny.

—SUSAN B. ANTHONY, A LEADER IN WOMAN SUFFRAGE, 1873

• • •

If you can keep your head when all about you
Are losing theirs and blaming it on you;
If you can trust yourself when all men doubt you,
But make allowance for their doubting too

• • •

Yours is the Earth and everything that's in it,
And—which is more—you'll be a Man my son!

—RUDYARD KIPLING, "IF"

• • •

Courage is needed for action. Knowing what to do without action is akin to Brownian motion, purposeless shaking in the same location. It is not leadership. Leadership is movement toward the goal.
—DJP, *ON LEADERSHIP*

• • •

Never mistake motion for action.
—ERNEST HEMINGWAY

• • •

I have been impressed with the urgency of doing. Knowing is not enough; we must apply. Being willing is not enough; we must do.
—LEONARDO DA VINCI

• • •

The person who embodies leadership for me is Nelson Mandela. Mandela inspired the world with his strength and courage in leading the fight against apartheid. . . . Many great leaders show courage, but Mandela, who was imprisoned for 27 years, coupled that courage with compassion and the ability to forgive.
—MELINDA FRENCH GATES, LETTER TO DJP, JUNE 25, 2007

• • •

A plan without action accomplishes nothing.
Think of Hurricane Katrina.

Leaders courageously lend a
helping hand to rescue others.

Our march to freedom is irreversible. We must not allow fear to stand in our way. Universal suffrage on a common voters' roll in a united democracy and non-racial South Africa is the only way to peace and racial harmony.

In conclusion I wish to quote my own words during my trial in 1964. They are as true today as they were then:

I have fought against white domination and I have fought against black domination. I have cherished the ideal of a democratic and free society in which all persons live together in harmony and with equal opportunities. It is an ideal which I hope to live for and to achieve. But if needs be, it is an ideal for which I am prepared to die.

—NELSON MANDELA FEBRUARY 11, 1990 AFTER RELEASE FROM PRISON

• • •

Courage is grace under pressure.

—ERNEST HEMINGWAY

• • •

When told the Germans had them surrounded during the Battle of the Bulge, U.S. General Creighton W. Abrams, Jr. stated: "They've got us surrounded again, the poor bastards." *And on December 22, 1944, the Germans sent a message to the Americans to surrender at Bastogne, and General McAuliffe's reply was* "Nuts". *The best the German translators could do with that was* "Go to Hell."
—FROM THE INFORMATION SUPPLIED TO ONONDAGA COUNTY MEDICAL SOCIETY, INC. BY DR. JACK T. PRIOR, WHO WAS A PHYSICIAN THERE DURING THE BATTLE.

• • •

We are a free country. Why are we? Because a lot of people—black, white, yellow—gave their lives so that you and I could live free. Simple as that.
—LEWIS MILLETT, MEDAL OF HONOR WINNER

• • •

Any man can shoot a gun, and with practice he can draw fast and shoot accurately, but that makes no difference. What counts is how you stand up when somebody is shooting back at you.
—LOUIS L'AMOUR

• • •

America has often served as a leader in promoting peace and democracy across the globe.

The communist type of totalitarian system has left both our nations, Czechs and Slovaks—as it has all the nations of the Soviet Union and the other countries the Soviet Union subjugated in its time—a legacy of countless dead, an infinite spectrum of human suffering, profound economic decline, and above all enormous human humiliation. It has brought us horrors that fortunately you have not known. . . .

When Thomas Jefferson wrote that "Governments are instituted among Men, deriving their just Powers from the Consent of the Governed," it was a simple and important act of the human spirit. What gave meaning to the act, however, was the fact that the author backed it up with his life. It was not just his words; it was his deeds as well.

—VÁCLAV HAVEL, ADDRESS TO A JOINT SESSION OF U.S. CONGRESS, FEBRUARY 21, 1990

• • •

An appeaser is one who feeds a crocodile, hoping that it will eat him last.

—WINSTON CHURCHILL

• • •

A statue of Winston Churchill that resides near Parliament in London, England.

P-51 "My Girl" Takes Off From Iwo Jima during WWII. Courage abounds in these American pilots in war. Image courtesy of National Library of Congress.

There is an outmoded Burmese proverb still recited by men who wish to deny that women too can play a part in bringing necessary change and progress to their society: "The dawn rises only when the rooster crows." But Burmese people today are well aware of the scientific reasons behind the rising of dawn and the falling of dusk. And the intelligent rooster surely realizes that it is because dawn comes that it crows and not the other way 'round. It crows to welcome the light that has come to relieve the darkness of night. It is not the prerogative of men alone to bring light to this world: women with their capacity for compassion and self-sacrifice, their courage and perseverance, have done much to dissipate the darkness of intolerance and hate, suffering and despair.
—DAW AUNG SAN SUU KYI (NOBEL PEACE PRIZE 1991), AUGUST 31, 1995 SPEECH

• • •

You will never do anything in this world without courage. It is
the greatest quality of the mind next to honor.
—ARISTOTLE

• • •

A supposed leader is a sham without courage.
—DJP, *ON LEADERSHIP*

• • •

I hold that it would be improper for any committee or any
employer to examine my conscience. They wouldn't know how
to get into it, they wouldn't know what to do when they got in
there, and I wouldn't let them in anyway. Like other Americans,
my acts and my words are open to inspection—not my thoughts
or my political affiliation.
—E.B. WHITE, AUTHOR OF *CHARLOTTE'S WEB*, IN A
NOVEMBER 29, 1947 LETTER TO *NEW YORK HERALD
TRIBUNE*

• • •

The statement "Never Missed a Performance" is an important element of leadership, embodying courage and reliability. Noted on April 15, 2012, at the Pride of Midtown, Engine 54, Ladder 4, Battalion 9, F.D.N.Y., at corner of 8th Avenue & W 48th St. Seventeen of these heroes made the supreme sacrifice on September 11, 2001 in the terrorist attack.

It takes courage to blaze your own path and proceed along the road less traveled.

Whatever course you decide upon, there is always someone to tell you that you are wrong. There are always difficulties arising which tempt you to believe that your critics are right. To map out a course of action and follow it to an end requires . . . courage.
—RALPH WALDO EMERSON

• • •

Let him not boast who puts his armor on as he who puts it off, the battle done.
—HENRY WADSWORTH LONGFELLOW

• • •

LESSONS LEARNED

- Courage is the fuel for leadership. There is no leadership without courage.

- Courage is not the absence of fear. Courage is acting in spite of fear.

- Naysayers and excuses for reasons not to act abound. Ignore them.

- Action is an essential ingredient for leadership, and courage starts the journey.

- Each of us has the opportunity to be courageous.

Preparation involves study, attention to detail, and work! When tired, think of the persistence of bees. ©1981 Donald J. Palmisano

6

Persistence: "Don't Give Up!"

Nothing in the world can take the place of persistence. Talent will not; nothing is more common than unsuccessful men with talent. Genius will not; unrewarded genius is almost a proverb. Education will not; the world is full of educated derelicts. Persistence and determination are omnipotent. The slogan "press on" has solved and always will solve the problems of the human race.
—CALVIN COOLIDGE

• • •

It is not easy to be a pioneer—but oh, it is fascinating! I would not trade one moment, even the worst moment, for all the riches in the world.
—ELIZABETH BLACKWELL, MD, FIRST WOMAN IN U.S.A. TO EARN MEDICAL DEGREE IN 1849

• • •

I decline to accept the end of man. It is easy enough to say that man is immortal simply because he will endure: that when the last ding-dong of doom has clanged and faded from the last worthless rock hanging tideless in the last red and dying evening, that even then there will still be one more sound: that of his puny inexhaustible voice, still talking. I refuse to accept this. I believe that man will not merely endure: he will prevail. He is immortal, not because he alone among creatures has an inexhaustible voice, but because he has a soul, a spirit capable of compassion and sacrifice and endurance. The poet's, the writer's, duty is to write about these things. It is his privilege to help man endure by lifting his heart, by reminding him of the courage and honor and hope and pride and compassion and pity and sacrifice which have been the glory of his past. The poet's voice need not merely be the record of man, it can be one of the props, the pillars to help him endure and prevail.
—WILLIAM FAULKNER, ON ACCEPTANCE OF NOBEL PRIZE FOR LITERATURE, DECEMBER 10, 1950

• • •

Go for it! Don't be limited by others' perceptions of you.

"Mr. Roark, we're alone here. Why don't you tell me what you think of me? In any words you wish. No one will hear us."
"But I don't think of you."
—CONVERSATION BETWEEN ELLSWORTH TOOHEY AND HOWARD ROARK IN *THE FOUNTAINHEAD* BY AYN RAND. (TWELVE PUBLISHERS REJECTED *THE FOUNTAINHEAD* BEFORE IT WAS ACCEPTED. THIS BOOK, AND HER SUBSEQUENT WRITINGS, INCLUDING *ATLAS SHRUGGED*, HAVE SOLD OVER 25 MILLION COPIES).

• • •

Of course, who cannot feel the power of Winston Churchill's persistence, when faced with the onslaught of Nazi Germany and the bombing of London in World War II? At that time, he said, "Never give in—never, never, never, never, in nothing great or small, large or petty, never give in except to convictions of honor and good sense. Never yield to force; never yield to the apparently overwhelming might of the enemy."
—*ON LEADERSHIP*

• • •

It's important for any leader to overcome rejection, in any form.

"I quit when medicine was placed under State control, some years ago," said Dr. Hendricks. "Do you know what it takes to perform a brain operation? Do you know the kind of skill it demands, and the years of passionate, merciless, excruciating devotion that go to acquire that skill? *That* was what I would not place at the disposal of men whose sole qualification to rule me was their capacity to spout the fraudulent generalities that got them elected to the privilege of enforcing their wishes at the point of a gun. I would not let them dictate the purpose for which my years of study had been spent, or the conditions of my work, or my choice of patients, or the amount of my reward. I observed that in all the discussions that preceded the enslavement of medicine, men discussed everything—except the desires of the doctors."

—DR. HENDRICKS IN *ATLAS SHRUGGED*,
1957 BY AYN RAND. COURTESY OF THE AYN RAND
INSTITUTE.

• • •

Sometimes responsibility can feel like the weight of the world.

Being black does not stop you. You can sit out in the world and say, "Well, white people kept me back, and I can't do this." Not so. You can have anything you want if you make up your mind and you want it.

—CLARA MCBRIDE HALE, FOUNDER OF HALE HOUSE FOR UNWANTED CHILDREN, INCLUDING THOSE WITH AIDS. PRESIDENT REAGAN, IN HIS JANUARY 1985 STATE OF THE UNION ADDRESS, CALLED HER AN AMERICAN HERO.

• • •

President Kennedy on May 25, 1961 set the goal in that decade of America landing a man on the moon and safely returning him to earth. John Houbolt conceived a method of Lunar Orbital Rendezvous (LOR) as a way to do it. The director of the Office of Space Flight Programs at NASA headquarters said, "I've been right most of my life about things, and if you guys are going to talk about rendezvous, any kind of rendezvous, as a way of going to the Moon, forget it. I've heard all those schemes and I don't want to hear any more of them, because we're not going to the Moon using any of those schemes." *Houbolt persisted, bypassed his bosses, and proved his method was the only way we could get to the Moon in the decade. LOR was the method used successfully.*

As NASA noted when quoting the 1982 view of George Low, a space pioneer and engineer, "It is my opinion to this day that had the Lunar Orbit Rendezvous Mode not been chosen, Apollo would not have succeeded."

—FULL STORY IN *ON LEADERSHIP* AND AT NASA

• • •

Mario Puzo's The Godfather *had multiple rejections before being accepted, and later the movie and its sequel,* The Godfather, Part II, *both won Academy Awards.*

As David Oshinsky wrote in the September 7, 2007, issue of The New York Times, The Diary of a Young Girl, *by Anne Frank, would be rejected by 15 publishers before Doubleday accepted it and published it in 1952. More than 30 million copies are currently in print, making it one of the best selling books in history.*

Oshinsky further points out that information, along with similar tales, are stored in the Knopf archive housed in the Harry Ransom Humanities Research Center at the University of Texas. Oshinsky states:

The document is one of thousands tucked away in the publisher's rejection files, a place where whopping editorial blunders are mercifully entombed. Nothing embarrasses a publisher more than the public knowledge that a literary classic or a mega best seller has somehow slipped away. One of them turned down Pearl Buck's novel "The Good Earth" on the grounds that Americans were "not interested in anything on China." Another passed on George Orwell's "Animal Farm," explaining it was "impossible to sell animal stories in the U.S.A."

—DJP

• • •

John C. Houbolt, July 24, 1962, showing his space rendezvous concept for lunar landings. Lunar Orbital Rendezvous (LOR) would be used in the Apollo program. (NASA image used with permission.)

Houston, Tranquility Base here. The Eagle has landed.
—NEIL ARMSTRONG, FIRST REPORT FROM MOON,
JULY 20, 1969

• • •

That's one small step for a man, one giant leap for mankind.
—NEIL ARMSTRONG, FIRST PERSON TO STAND ON
MOON, JULY 20, 1969

• • •

Facts don't cease to exist because they are ignored.
—ALDOUS HUXLEY

• • •

Always tell the truth. That way, you never have to wonder what
answer you gave; just always be truthful. I have MS; it does not
have me.
—JEROME GOLDSTEIN, MD, FORMER EVP, AMERICAN
ACADEMY OF OTOLARYNGOLOGY-HEAD AND NECK
SURGERY

• • •

In imagination I can hear Homer singing, as with unsteady, hesitating steps he gropes his way from camp to camp—singing of life, of love, of war, of the splendid achievements of a noble race. It was a wonderful, glorious song, and it won the blind poet an immortal crown, the admiration of all ages.
—HELEN KELLER, WHO GREW UP BLIND AND DEAF,
THE STORY OF MY LIFE

• • •

LESSONS LEARNED

- Genius and talent amount to naught if one doesn't persist in pursuit of the goal.

- Persistence doesn't mean blind repetition when failure occurs. It does mean analysis to see if the conclusion or approach is correct and if so, pursuing that approach. If changes need to be made, do so, and continue on.

- Draw encouragement from stories that show how persistence leads to success. Search for more stories. Every such story contains a lesson for those whose minds remain open to new ideas.

Helen Keller, blind and deaf since childhood, and her teacher Anne Sullivan are an inspiration to all who aspire to leadership. Read Helen Keller's amazing story in her autobiography.

Timely decision-making is an absolute requirement of leadership.

7

Decisiveness

The person who in shaky times also wavers only increases the
evil, but the person of firm decision fashions the universe.
—JOHANN WOLFGANG VON GOETHE

• • •

The most difficult thing is the decision to act, the rest is merely
tenacity. The fears are paper tigers. You can do anything you
decide to do. You can act to change and control your life; and the
procedure; the process is its own reward.
—AMELIA EARHART, FIRST WOMAN TO FLY SOLO
ACROSS THE ATLANTIC OCEAN

• • •

In any moment of decision the best thing you can do is the right thing, the next best thing is the wrong thing, and the worst thing you can do is nothing.
—PRESIDENT THEODORE ROOSEVELT

• • •

Indecision and delays are parents of failure.
—GEORGE CANNING, NINETEENTH CENTURY BRITISH STATESMAN

• • •

Ideas are a dime a dozen but implementation is everything. We need a Quiet Revolution Back to Basics.
—JOHN BOGLE, *THE CLASH OF THE CULTURES: INVESTMENT VS. SPECULATION*

• • •

Lest we forget: Many in the military have paid the ultimate price for our freedom.

I address you with neither rancor nor bitterness in the fading twilight of life, with but one purpose in mind: to serve my country. . . .

But once war is forced upon us, there is no other alternative than to apply every available means to bring it to a swift end.

War's very object is victory, not prolonged indecision.

In war there is no substitute for victory.

There are some who, for varying reasons, would appease Red China. They are blind to history's clear lesson, for history teaches with unmistakable emphasis that appeasement but begets new and bloodier war. It points to no single instance where this end has justified that means, where appeasement has led to more than a sham peace. Like blackmail, it lays the basis for new and successively greater demands until, as in blackmail, violence becomes the only other alternative.

"Why," my soldiers asked of me, "surrender military advantages to an enemy in the field?" I could not answer.

Of the nations of the world, Korea alone, up to now, is the sole one which has risked its all against communism. The magnificence of the courage and fortitude of the Korean people defies description.

Continued...

They have chosen to risk death rather than slavery. Their last words to me were: "Don't scuttle the Pacific!"

I have just left your fighting sons in Korea. They have met all tests there, and I can report to you without reservation that they are splendid in every way. . . .

I am closing my 52 years of military service. When I joined the Army, even before the turn of the century, it was the fulfillment of all of my boyish hopes and dreams. The world has turned over many times since I took the oath on the plain at West Point, and the hopes and dreams have long since vanished, but I still remember the refrain of one of the most popular barrack ballads of that day which proclaimed most proudly that "old soldiers never die; they just fade away."

And like the old soldier of that ballad, I now close my military career and just fade away, an old soldier who tried to do his duty as God gave him the light to see that duty.

Good Bye.

—GENERAL DOUGLAS MACARTHUR SPEECH, TO CON-GRESS AFTER BEING RELIEVED OF DUTY BY PRESIDENT TRUMAN, APRIL 19, 1951

• • •

Indecision can be crippling for a leader.

LESSONS LEARNED

- To be a leader, one must make timely decisions.

- Fear is the root cause of indecision.

- Fear stems from a dread of being blamed if failure ensues.

- Indecision and delays beget failure.

- Learn that the consequences of indecision bring long-term lack of respect and can cause the death of others who depend on the person in authority.

- Make a timely decision and move on. There will always be those who criticize once the results are known. Usually, hindsight bias is their only tool.

- Take responsibility for your decisions and actions.

- Anticipate what could go wrong and be prepared.

- Practice "what-if" scenarios to condition your mind to act in a crisis, even if the crisis puts you at risk.

- The best plan is worthless without the decision to act.

Communication takes many forms.

8

Communication

The great enemy of clear language is insincerity. When there is a gap between one's real and one's declared aims, one turns, as it were, instinctively to long words and exhausted idioms, like a cuttlefish squirting out ink.
—GEORGE ORWELL

• • •

The newest computer can merely compound, at speed, the oldest problem in the relations between human beings, and in the end the communicator will be confronted with the old problem, of what to say and how to say it.

—EDWARD R. MURROW

• • •

Ecclesiastes: I returned, and saw under the sun, that the race is not to the swift, nor the battle to the strong, neither yet bread to the wise, not yet riches to men of understanding, nor yet favor to men of skill; but time and chance happeneth to them all.
Compare to Modern English:
Objective consideration of contemporary phenomena compels the conclusion that success or failure in competitive activities exhibits no tendency to be commensurate with innate capacity, but that a considerable element of the unpredictable must invariably be taken into account.
—GEORGE ORWELL QUOTED IN STRUNK AND WHITE'S *ELEMENTS OF STYLE* AND IN *ON LEADERSHIP*

• • •

The difference between the right word and the almost right word is the difference between lightning and the lightning bug.
—MARK TWAIN

• • •

To sing, to laugh, to dream,
To walk in my own way and be alone,
Free, with an eye to see things as they are,
A voice that means manhood . . .
—BRIAN HOOKER TRANSLATION OF *CYRANO DE BERGERAC* BY EDMOND ROSTAND

• • •

Clear, honest communication is essential for building trust both in the workplace and in life. It's hard to lead if you can't be trusted.

There has never been a nation like #America or a people like #Americans. It is an inspiration to all the world. . . .
—U.S. SENATOR MARCO RUBIO TWEET AT @MARCORUBIO, JULY 31, 2011

• • •

For years, my dad would work banquets at hotels. At these events there are usually only two people standing—the speaker on the podium and the bartender behind the bar. My dad was the one behind the bar. But he worked all his life so that his kids could make the symbolic journey from the bar to the podium. That journey is a testament to the greatness of America.
—SENATOR MARCO RUBIO, FROM HIS AUTOBIOGRAPHY, *AN AMERICAN SON*

• • •

Whether speaking to the Senate or to the humblest person, use language that is respectful, but not affected. Let your speech be plain and honest.
—MARCUS AURELIUS, *MEDITATIONS,* TRANSLATED BY C. SCOT HICKS AND DAVID V. HICKS, *THE EMPEROR'S HANDBOOK*

• • •

Whate'er is well conceived is clearly said, and the words to say it
flow with ease.
—NICHOLAS BOILEAU-DESPREAUX, 1636-1711

• • •

The secret of being a bore is to tell everything.
—VOLTAIRE, 1694-1778

• • •

Master rhetoric, and you have mastered persuasion. Persuade,
and you have gone a long way toward mastering your social
environment.
—WILLARD R. ESPY, *THE GARDEN OF ELOQUENCE*

• • •

I have made this letter longer than usual, because I lack the time
to make it short.
—BLAISE PASCAL

• • •

Is life so dear, or peace so sweet, as to be purchased at the price of chains and slavery? Forbid it, Almighty God!
I know not what course others may take; but as for me, *give me liberty or give me death*!
—PATRICK HENRY, 1775

• • •

I have a dream that my four little children will one day live in a nation where they will not be judged by the color of their skin but by the content of their character.
 . . . When we let freedom ring, when we let it ring from every village and every hamlet, from every state and every city, we will be able to speed up that day when all of God's children, black men and white men, Jews and Gentiles, Protestants and Catholics, will be able to join hands and sing in the words of the old Negro spiritual, "Free at last! Free at last! Thank God Almighty, we are free at last!"
—MARTIN LUTHER KING, JR., SPEECH, "I HAVE A DREAM," LINCOLN MEMORIAL, WASHINGTON, D.C., AUGUST 28, 1963

• • •

Enlighten the people generally, and tyranny and oppressions of body and mind will vanish like evil spirits at the dawn of day.
—THOMAS JEFFERSON

• • •

Martin Luther King Jr. monument in
Washington, D.C.

I served with General Washington in the Legislature of Virginia before the Revolution and, during it, with Dr. Franklin in Congress. I never heard either of them speak ten minutes at a time, nor to any but the main point which was to decide the question. They laid their shoulders to the great points, knowing that the little ones would follow of themselves.
—THOMAS JEFFERSON

• • •

I am aware that many object to the severity of my language; but is there not cause for severity? I will be as harsh as truth, and as uncompromising as justice. On this subject, I do not wish to think, or to speak, or write, with moderation. No! No! Tell a man whose house is on fire to give a moderate alarm; tell him to moderately rescue his wife from the hands of the ravisher; tell the mother to gradually extricate her babe from the fire into which it has fallen; — but urge me not to use moderation in a cause like the present. I am in earnest — I will not equivocate — I will not excuse — I will not retreat a single inch — AND I WILL BE HEARD. The apathy of the people is enough to make every statue leap from its pedestal, and to hasten the resurrection of the dead.
—WILLIAM LLOYD GARRISON, *THE LIBERATOR,* JANUARY 1, 1831

• • •

The Thomas Jefferson memorial in Washington, D.C.

. . . So let us begin anew—remembering on both sides that civility is not a sign of weakness, and sincerity is always subject to proof. Let us never negotiate out of fear. But let us never fear to negotiate. . . . And so, my fellow Americans: ask not what your country can do for you—ask what you can do you can do for your country. . . . My fellow citizens of the world: ask not what America will do for you, but what together we can do for the freedom of man.
—PRESIDENT JOHN F. KENNEDY'S INAUGURAL ADDRESS, JANUARY 20, 1961

• • •

Important factors in delivering good speeches are preparation and knowledge of both your subject and the group you'll be addressing. Be honest, be straightforward. Think in terms of words and phrases that people can understand. It is important for leaders to be sufficiently well prepared to allow them to focus attention on the people they are talking to.
—EDWARD ANNIS, MD, A LEGEND AS AMA PRESIDENT. *ON LEADERSHIP*

• • •

LESSONS LEARNED

- Clear, unequivocal communication is necessary for strong leadership.

- A well-prepared, written message is less likely to be distorted by others.

- Great speeches of the past are a good place to learn about content, organization, and delivery.

- Learning rhetorical devices will make you a more effective writer and speaker.

- Preparation is the key for interviews and debates.

- Remain on topic during interviews.

- Practice makes perfect. Have notes available if your mind goes blank.

- Meetings can be a waste of time, but if led properly, they can effect positive change.

- Knowing parliamentary procedure will help you to advance your ideas.

- Carefully monitoring the minutes of a meeting can prevent errors. The person who controls the minutes controls the future of the organization.

Without creativity, the world would not progress. Leaders use creativity to achieve goals.

9

Creativity and Acquiring the
State of Mind Necessary for
Success

Many highly intelligent people are poor thinkers. Many people
of average intelligence are skilled thinkers. The power of a car is
separate from the way the car is driven.
—EDWARD DE BONO

• • •

The ultimate measure of a man is not where he stands in
moments of comfort and convenience, but where he stands at
times of challenge and controversy.
—MARTIN LUTHER KING, JR.

• • •

The subtlest change in New York is something people don't speak much about but that is in everyone's mind. The city, for the first time in its long history, is destructible. A single flight of planes no bigger than a wedge of geese can quickly end this island fantasy, burn the towers, crumble the bridges, turn the underground passages into lethal chambers, cremate the millions. The intimation of mortality is part of New York now: in the sound of jets overhead, in the black headlines of the latest edition.

All dwellers in cities must live with the stubborn fact of annihilation; in New York the fact is somewhat more concentrated because of the concentration of the city itself, and because, of all targets, New York has a certain clear priority. In the mind of whatever perverted dreamer might loose the lightning, New York must hold a steady irresistible charm.

—E.B. WHITE, *HERE IS NEW YORK*, 1949

• • •

An essential aspect of creativity is not being afraid to fail.
—EDWARD LAND, INVENTOR OF THE POLAROID CAMERA

• • •

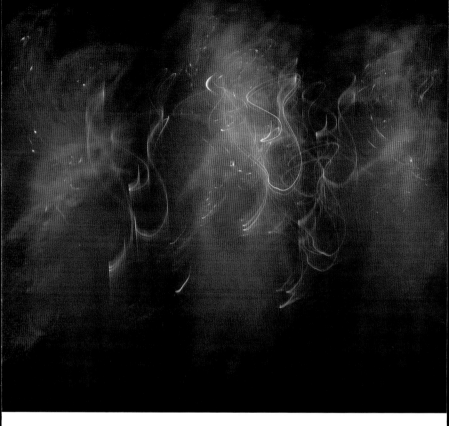

Creativity frequently involves experimentation. Here 3 women fiddlers in Australia were captured as aura by painting with light using a camera. Image selected for cover of the Journal of the Louisiana State Medical Society March/April 2011. ©2009 Donald J. Palmisano.

Creativity illuminates the path.

Creativity is a great motivator because it makes people interested in what they are doing. Creativity gives hope that there can be a worthwhile idea. Creativity gives the possibility of some sort of achievement to everyone. Creativity makes life more fun and more interesting.
—EDWARD DE BONO, AUTHOR OF *NEW THINK*

• • •

The creative person is a risk taker, but carefully considers what could go wrong and is prepared to deal with the complications. The leader learns from failure and tries to understand the system that set a person up for error rather than looking for scapegoats. Failure to fix the system means the error will occur again with someone else.
—DJP, *ON LEADERSHIP*

• • •

Imagination is more important than knowledge. For while knowledge defines all we currently know and understand, imagination points to all we might yet discover and create.
—ALBERT EINSTEIN

• • •

109

Success four flights Thursday morning all against twenty one mile wind started from Level with engine power alone average speed through air thirty one miles longest 57 seconds inform Press home Christmas.
—ORVILLE WRIGHT'S TELEGRAM ANNOUNCING THE WORLD'S FIRST POWERED FLIGHT, DECEMBER 17, 1903

• • •

Great discoveries frequently are made by new voices and contrarians. Leaders are not afraid of failure.
—DJP, *ON LEADERSHIP*

• • •

LESSONS LEARNED

- Intelligence is important in leadership, but skilled thinking is critical.

- Fostering creativity is an important enhancement to logical thinking.

- A state of mind that welcomes curiosity, tries new approaches, and learns from error is a favorable approach to leadership development.

- Reading books on creativity generates new ideas and expands innovative possibilities.

- Always consider alternative paths to the same destination.

- A person who courageously seeks a new path is easily distinguished from the crowd.

- Leaders are not afraid of failure; they see it as a teaching experience.

- Leaders focus and do not waste time on unimportant activity.

"An An," the Giant Panda, whose name means Peace. After DJP gave a lecture in Shanghai in 2007, he was asked if there was anything special he wished to see or do. DJP requested a visit to a Giant Panda and here is his photo of An An. Sharing interests opens lines of communication, and leaders frequently use mutual interests to foster better relationships.

10

Interpersonal Relationships

Piglet sidled up to Pooh from behind. "Pooh!" he whispered.
"Yes, Piglet?" "Nothing," said Piglet, taking Pooh's paw. "I just
wanted to be sure of you."
—A.A. MILNE

• • •

My bounty is as boundless as the sea.
My love as deep. The more I give to thee
The more I have, for both are infinite.
—WILLIAM SHAKESPEARE, *ROMEO AND JULIET*

• • •

Let me not to the marriage of true minds
Admit impediments. Love is not love
Which alters when it alteration finds,
Or bends with the remover to remove.
O, no! It is an ever-fixed mark
That looks on tempests and is never shaken;
It is the star to every wand'ring bark,
Whose worth's unknown, although his height be taken.
Love's not Time's fool, though rosy lips and cheeks
Within his bending sickle's compass come;
Love alters not with his brief hours and weeks,
But bears it out even to the edge of doom.
If this be error and upon me proved,
I never writ, nor no man ever loved.
—WILLIAM SHAKESPEARE, "SONNET 116"

• • •

Leaders don't point fingers and blame others. Leaders get the job
done; when problems arise, they find the source and fix it.

It is important to be respectful and civil. This does not mean succumbing to intimidation. Never respond in kind to name-calling. Stick to the issue in a logical unemotional way. That is one of the paths to leadership.

Despite these cautions, never forget that some people crave power and believe their feelings of poor self-worth can be overcome by exercising power over others and having their names emblazoned on buildings. They fail to learn the lessons of history, like the one captured in Percy Bysshe Shelley's poignant 1818 poem, "Ozymandias":

I met a traveller from an antique land
Who said: Two vast and trunkless legs of stone
Stand in the desert. Near them on the sand,
Half sunk, a shatter'd visage lies, whose frown
And wrinkled lip and sneer of cold command
Tell that its sculptor well those passions read
Which yet survive, stamp'd on these lifeless things,
The hand that mock'd them and the heart that fed.
And on the pedestal these words appear:
"My name is Ozymandias, king of kings:
Look on my works, ye mighty, and despair!"
Nothing beside remains: round the decay
Of that colossal wreck, boundless and bare,
The lone and level sands stretch far away.
—PERCY BYSSHE SHELLEY, "OZYMANDIAS" AND
TEXT FROM *ON LEADERSHIP*

• • •

Hong Kong 2007 view from Victoria Peak in this photo DJP captured on a borrowed tripod from the person standing next to DJP. With travel, learning occurs and relationships are enhanced with locals when you learn some of their language and always smile!

In prosperity our friends know us; in adversity we know our friends.
—JOHN CHURTON COLLINS, 1848-1908

• • •

Every time you smile at someone, it is an action of love, a gift to that person, a beautiful thing.
—MOTHER TERESA, NOBEL PEACE PRIZE RECIPIENT, 1979

• • •

Nearly all men can stand adversity, but if you want to test a man's character, give him power.
—ABRAHAM LINCOLN

• • •

"It doesn't *matter* that you never got caught!"

Leaders must be ethical!

"Until this moment, Senator, I think I never really gauged your cruelty or your recklessness." When McCarthy tried to continue his attack, Welch angrily interrupted, "Let us not assassinate this lad further, senator. You have done enough. Have you no sense of decency?"
—ARMY ATTORNEY JOSEPH N. WELCH TO SENATOR JOSEPH J. MCCARTHY, TELEVISED ARMY-MCCARTHY HEARINGS; JUNE 9, 1954, U.S. SENATE ARCHIVES.

• • •

Advice to young doctors: As you start your professional journey it is important to have a method of navigation—the equivalent of a North Star, a compass, a global positioning satellite system.
I believe that system can be remembered with the acronym SEC-C. Not SEXY—S-E-X-Y—but S-E-C-C.
And that stands for: Science – Ethics–Compassion – Courage.
These are the cornerstones for a foundation that will keep you true to your calling, the pursuit of knowledge and the translation of that knowledge into healing and comfort for your patients.
These four words tell you what you need to do, what you can do, and what you will do. When in doubt, return to them for your bearings, for hope, and for strength.
These four words will remind you, inspire you, and give you solace when you are alone with a patient who is slipping away to the beyond.

Continued...

Remembering these four words, Science – Ethics – Compassion – Courage, and combining them with two sentences is your equivalent of the commandments of Medicine. The two sentences are:

- Is this in the patient's best interest?

- Do I have my patient's informed consent?

If you accomplish this, you will be true to your patient and to yourself.

—DJP ON THE 6 SIX COMMANDMENTS OF MEDICINE, COMMENCEMENT SPEECH LSU HEALTH SCIENCES CENTER, MAY 18, 2002

• • •

Remember: Short-term gains or Pyrrhic victories are not the goals of a loving marriage or a friendship. Refusal to listen, correcting errors made during an emotional upset, or trying to win with "scorched earth" retaliation is destructive to a long-term relationship. Win-win is the aspirational ideal, and compassionate communication is the means to that end.

—ON LEADERSHIP

• • •

The meeting of two personalities is like the contact of two chemical substances: if there is any reaction, both are transformed.

—C.G. JUNG

• • •

Thousands of life-size terracotta figures of warriors and horses from 211-206 BC at the Emperor Qin Shi Huang's Mausoleum in Xi'an, China. Individuals digging a well in 1974 discovered them accidently and excavation began soon after. Is the past prologue for the future?

Indifference and neglect often do much more damage than out-right dislike.
—J.K. ROWLING, *HARRY POTTER AND THE ORDER OF THE PHOENIX*

• • •

LESSONS LEARNED

- Remember the three critical points of compassionate communication:

  1. Learn to be an active listener.
  2. Validate the feelings of others in a discussion.
  3. Ask how you can help after listening to someone who is upset.

- Before any meeting with your boss attended by others, alert him or her to any facts that are critical to issues on the agenda.

- Practice civility but never compromise your principles.
- Never lose the common touch by letting status change you.

- Learn to distinguish between friends and opportunists.
- Select associates on merit and always verify credentials from primary sources.

- Physicians should remember the 6 commandments of medicine.

This statue remembers the Katyn Massacre of 1940, where over 20,000 Polish nationals were murdered by Soviet Secret Police on Stalin's order. This is another example of a non-leader who spread lies. The statue is in Jersey City, New Jersey. Photo courtesy of DJP.

11

Finding Truth

In a time of universal deceit, telling the truth becomes a revolu-
tionary act.
—George Orwell

The devil can cite Scripture for his purpose.
An evil soul producing holy witness
Is like a villain with a smiling cheek,
A goodly apple rotten at the heart.
O, what a goodly outside falsehood hath!
—WILLIAM SHAKESPEARE, ANTONIO IN *THE
MERCHANT OF VENICE*

• • •

The liar is no whit better than the thief, and if his mendacity takes the form of slander, he may be worse than most thieves.
—THEODORE ROOSEVELT

• • •

✠   Winners take responsibility. Losers blame others.
—BRIT HUME MARCH 18, 2012, FOX NEWS SUNDAY

• • •

When a trial lawyer asks a witness a question, he is trying to destroy the credibility of the opposition witness. After asking the question he may read a conflicting statement the witness made earlier in a deposition and ask, "Are you lying now or when you gave the deposition?" Many trial lawyers tell me the goal in a trial is to win, not to find the truth, and that truth is what the jury says it is.
—*ON LEADERSHIP*

• • •

I would sooner trust the smallest slip of paper for truth, than the strongest and most retentive memory, ever bestowed on mortal man.
—JUSTICE LUMPKIN, J., MILLER V COTTON, 5 GA 341, 349 (1848)

• • •

One of the most profound observations on statistics is attributed by Mark Twain to nineteenth century British Prime Minister Benjamin Disraeli. Twain writes: "Figures often beguile me, particularly when I have the arranging of them myself; in which case the remark attributed to Disraeli would often apply with justice and force: 'There are three kinds of lies: lies, damned lies, and statistics.'"
—*ON LEADERSHIP*

• • •

Few lies carry the inventor's mark; and the most prostitute enemy to truth may spread a thousand without being known for the author. Besides, as the vilest writer hath his readers, so the greatest liar hath his believers; and it often happens that, if a lie be believed only for an hour, it hath done its work, and there is no farther occasion for it. Falsehood flies, and Truth comes limping after it, so that when men come to be undeceived, it is too late; the jest is over, and the tale hath had its effect: like a man who hath thought of a good repartee when the discourse is changed or the company parted; or like a physician who hath found out an infallible medicine after the patient is dead.
—JONATHAN SWIFT, *THE ART OF POLITICAL LYING*

• • •

Finding Truth

Leaders must not only tell the truth but also pursue the truth when others conceal it. It is not an easy task but this is an important distinguishing feature of a leader. The pursuit of truth in the political arena is most challenging. As I listen to claims and counterclaims and spinmasters on television, I am reminded of George Orwell's dystopian novel, *Nineteen Eighty-Four* wherein the main character Winston Smith lives in a totalitarian state and works in the "Ministry of Truth." In that place history constantly is rewritten and evidence destroyed. Progress never will occur with such activity. Freedom, liberty, the rule of law, and truth are the keys to progress. Without truth, a people, a state, a country withers like a plant without water. As Winston Churchill said, "The truth is incontrovertible. Malice may attack it and ignorance may deride it, but in the end there it is." It is up to leaders to seek it out. The electorate cries out for such authentic leadership.

—*ON LEADERSHIP*

• • •

Truth is a hallmark of leadership. The U.S.A. would be a better place with less "spin" and more truth in Congress.

Andrew Breitbart & DJP presenting at 10-20-2009 bloggers briefing
at Heritage Foundation. Photo courtesy of Don Irvine.

I love my job. I love fighting for what I believe in. I love having fun while doing it. I love reporting stories that the Complex refuses to report. I love fighting back, I love finding allies, and—famously—I enjoy making enemies.
—ANDREW BREITBART, DIED MARCH 1, 2012 AT AGE 43

• • •

Andrew was incredibly kind, devoted to his family and work, and most importantly, enthusiastic about life. He was certainly an inspiration to me personally and to countless others who have become reporters, bloggers, or activists in search of the truth.
—ROB BLUEY, HERITAGE FOUNDATION, MARCH 1, 2012

• • •

Farewell to Andrew Breitbart—the most fearless person I've ever known. . . . Losing him is like a fiery planet going dark.
—GREG GUTFELD, HOST OF *RED EYE* AND CO-HOST OF *THE FIVE* ON FOX NEWS, MARCH 1, 2012

• • •

Imagination should give wings to our thoughts, but we always need decisive experimental proof . . .
—LOUIS PASTEUR

• • •

The CATO Rule by DJP: Complete, Accurate, Timely, and Objective

Medical records continue to be one of the most important items in malpractice litigation. Because we don't have the time machine of H.G. Wells to take us back in time to determine exactly what happened, the medical record is considered the best witness to the past. Memories fade, people lie, witnesses die, but the medical record lives on. It should be complete, accurate, timely completed, and objective. Avoid subjective comments or name-calling. Imagine whatever you write being published in the newspaper.

—DJP, 1989 MEDICAL RISK MANAGER NEWSLETTER, HAWAII EDITION

• • •

Persuade me or prove to me that I am mistaken in thought or deed, and I will gladly change—for it is the truth I seek, and the truth never harmed anyone. Harm comes from persisting in error and clinging to ignorance.

—MARCUS AURELIUS, *MEDITATIONS,* TRANSLATED BY C. SCOT HICKS AND DAVID V. HICKS, *THE EMPEROR'S HANDBOOK*

• • •

Truth, the mother of justice.
—COKE, *SECOND INSTITUTE,* 524

• • •

This stamp depicts the chemist and microbiologist Louis Pasteur at work. It was through his creativity and rigor that he achieved a major breakthrough in the causes and preventions of diseases.

Human behaviour reveals uniformities which constitute natural laws. If these uniformities did not exist, then there would be neither social science nor political economy, and even the study of history would largely be useless. In effect, if the future actions of men having nothing in common with their past actions, our knowledge of them, although possibly satisfying our curiosity by way of an interesting story, would be entirely useless to us as a guide in life.
—VILFREDO PARETO, *COURS D'ECONOMIE POLITIQUE* (1896-7), VOL. 2, 397.

• • •

Get an understanding of statistics so you can evaluate data presented to you and discern when the conclusions are not based on the evidence. Also, helpful rules such as the Pareto principle (80-20 rule or law of the vital few), developed from the research of Vilredo Pareto, the Italian economist, focus your efforts on the 80% of effects from 20% of the causes.
—DJP

• • •

Imagine a world in which our medical liability system supported healing, education and innovation, instead of breeding fear, suffering and mistrust.

Now consider the cruel reality of a system that doesn't accurately judge negligence, that decreases quality and access to care, and increases the cost of medical care.

Take, for instance, the cost of defensive medicine—those additional tests and procedures performed from fear of a lawsuit, and not to help a patient.

It's not enough just to practice solid, evidence-based medicine. Physicians now are also forced to anticipate what lawyers might ask in courtroom interrogations—and to consider what claims could be made by medical witnesses for hire.

President Bush, who has been a vocal supporter of medical liability reform, put it this way: "If you think you're going to get sued, you do everything you can to prevent the trial lawyer from coming after you."

But defensive medicine translates into more procedures and tests, more patient discomfort and risk and—again—higher costs.

This sad state of affairs is largely the creation of a cadre of trial lawyers who are choking the health care system. They operate without any decent restraint, and are not held accountable for filing even the most worthless complaint.

On any given day, more than 125,000 cases against physicians clog our nation's courts. Think about that! Yet 70 percent of those filed are closed with no payment — and physicians win 80 percent of the cases that do go to trial.

—DJP, AMA PRESIDENT, NATIONAL PRESS CLUB NEWSMAKER LUNCHEON, WASHINGTON, D.C., JULY 9, 2003

• • •

Adolph Hitler was an evil man, a mass murderer, and the antithesis of truth. He was not a true leader despite having immense power. He was a liar and a racist who ruled by coercion, fear, and murder. Image courtesy of National Library of Congress.

The passing of W. Edwards Deming is a milestone event for the world of quality. We have all lost a useful, dedicated contributor to progress in the field. We have been privileged to witness a dedicated professional, fully absorbed in his mission despite personal tragedies, despite old age, and despite serious illness, yet giving freely of his time even when he had little time left to give. For that privilege, we should all be grateful.

—JOSEPH M. JURAN

• • •

LESSONS LEARNED

- Leaders are truthful. Pursue truth no matter how difficult the task.

- Timely documentation of events decreases the risk of disputes later as to what really happened.

- In the quest for truth, don't let others frame the debate or limit it.

- Obtaining truth and fixing flawed systems does more good than "shame and blame."

- Verify information from Internet sources because errors abound.

- Gain a working knowledge of statistics so you can identify misleading or statistical conclusions with bias.

- Being truthful earns respect and credibility and gathers followers.

A good fiduciary knows the finances and the mission.

12

Financial Considerations and Fiduciary Responsibility

To deal with conflicts of interest, an area that requires special vigilance by board members, the American Bar Association stipulates three rules for nonprofit corporations: awareness, disclosure, and disinterested review.
—ON LEADERSHIP

• • •

Non-profit directors have the three commonly recognized duties to the organization: the duties of CARE (of a prudent person), LOYALTY (to interests of organization), and OBEDIENCE (to mission of organization).
—ON LEADERSHIP QUOTING *BOARD LIABILITY* BY DANIEL L. KURTZ

• • •

With great power comes great responsibility.
—SPIDER-MAN'S UNCLE BEN

• • •

A business leader must focus on cash, control, and communication: cash to be sure the company stays solvent; control that ensures focus on internal checks and balances; and communication, both internal and external.
—EUGENE M. BULLIS, RETIRED BUSINESS TURNAROUND EXECUTIVE

• • •

In response to the admonition that we must move fast or lose the opportunity: Our duty is to act with prudence and to do a risk/benefit analysis after a good-faith effort to research the facts. To paraphrase Francis Bacon, the slower man who keeps the right road accomplishes the mission faster than the fast runner who takes a wrong road in haste.
—*ON LEADERSHIP*

• • •

*Don't take shortcuts; take your time & follow your plan or path & you'll achieve your goal in time.

High-tech portable gadgets enhance rapid retrieval of critical information necessary for decision-making.

Board service requires homework and attention to details.

Advice to DJP from his dad as they drove past a racetrack: "Son, the people who hang out here will end up barefoot in the winter and wearing old overcoats in the summer."
—*ON LEADERSHIP*

• • •

A man with a surplus can control circumstances, but a man without a surplus is controlled by them, and often has no opportunity to exercise judgment.
—HARVEY SAMUEL FIRESTONE

• • •

If past history was all there was to the game, the richest people would be librarians.
—WARREN BUFFETT

• • •

Annual income twenty pounds, annual expenditure nineteen six, result happiness. Annual income twenty pounds, annual expenditure twenty pound ought and six, result misery.
—CHARLES DICKENS

• • •

When the well runs dry, we all know the worth of water.
—BEN FRANKLIN

• • •

Wishes cost nothing, unless you want them to come true.
— FRANK TYGER

• • •

Price is what you pay. Value is what you get.
—WARREN BUFFETT

• • •

Safeguarding the money in business and timely use of it for the mission of the business is important. If only the government understood that concept, we would pay fewer taxes and not have deficits.

Don't waste money. No money, no mission.

STOP SPENDING

PRINTING $ WASTING !

LESSONS LEARNED

- Learn basic accounting and investing analysis for service on a board.

- Understand clearly fiduciary responsibilities, whether a board member or someone in public service, including Congress.

- Before introducing a proposal at a meeting, be prepared to present evidence that its advantages outweigh its risks. Also affirm that the proposal's purpose is relevant to the organization's mission.

Beauty in China 2007.
Travel introduces you
to different cultures
and languages and
one soon realizes
that the smile is a
universal sign of
friendship.

13

Expanding Your Horizons

Travel is fatal to prejudice, bigotry, and narrow-mindedness,
and many of our people need it sorely on these accounts. Broad,
wholesome, charitable views of men and things cannot be acquired
by vegetating in one little corner of the earth all one's lifetime.
—MARK TWAIN

• • •

Reading maketh a full man; conference a ready man; and writing
an exact man.
—SIR FRANCIS BACON

• • •

The man who does not read good books has no advantage over
the man who can't read them.
—MARK TWAIN

• • •

Statement at New York City Public Library.

The world of books is the most remarkable creation of man. Nothing else that he builds ever lasts. Monuments fall, nations perish, civilizations grow old and die out and after an era of darkness new races build others. But in the world of books are volumes that have seen this happen again and again and yet live on, still young, still as fresh as the day they were written, still telling men's hearts of men centuries dead.
—CLARENCE DAY

• • •

During one of my trips to China, a student asked me if I had heard of the novel *To Kill a Mockingbird.* I said yes, and he replied, "That is my favorite book." Once again, I saw the power of words. Words mean something.
—DJP, *ON LEADERSHIP*

• • •

In June 2003, the Chairman of the British Medical Association characterized his nation's single-payer health care system as "the stifling of innovation by excessive, intrusive audit . . . the shackling of doctors by prescribing guidelines, referral guidelines and protocols . . . the suffocation of professional responsibility by target-setting and production-line values that leave little room for the professional judgment of individual doctors or the needs of individual patients." His strong words come from long experience with a single-payer health system.
—EXCERPT FROM DECEMBER 3, 2003 COMMENT BY AMA PRESIDENT PALMISANO, DJ, IN JAMA 290 (21): 2797, AFTER TRAVELING TO ENGLAND AND ATTENDING THE BMA ANNUAL MEETING

• • •

Nothing is more powerful than an idea whose time has come.
—VICTOR HUGO, AUTHOR OF *LES MISERABLES*

• • •

These are the times that try men's souls. The summer soldier and the sunshine patriot will, in this crisis, shrink from the service of his country; but he that stands it now, deserves the love and thanks of man and woman.

Tyranny, like hell, is not easily conquered; yet we have this consolation with us, that the harder the conflict, the more glorious the triumph. What we obtain too cheap, we esteem too lightly; 'Tis dearness only that gives everything its value. Heaven knows how to put a proper price upon its goods; and it would be strange indeed if so celestial an article as Freedom should not be highly rated.
—THOMAS PAINE *THE CRISIS*; GENERAL WASHINGTON HAD THIS READ TO HIS SOLDIERS AFTER THE RETREAT FROM FORT LEE

• • •

The real price of everything is the toil and trouble of acquiring it.
—ADAM SMITH

• • •

Overcoming challenges; without dreams, no progress.

Washington & Lafayette at Valley Forge—Courtesy of Library of
Congress.

Take a moment from the stress of each day and reflect on ways to create new wealth and enrich yourself and the world: It is a socialist idea that making profits is a vice. I consider the real vice is making losses.
—WINSTON CHURCHILL

• • •

Those who love deeply never grow old; they may die of old age, but they die young.
—SIR ARTHUR WING PINERO

• • •

A man that seeks truth and loves it must be reckoned precious to any human society.
—FREDERICK THE GREAT

• • •

Whenever you commend, add your reasons for doing so; it is this which distinguishes the approbation of a man of sense from the flattery of sycophants and admiration of fools.
—RICHARD STEELE

• • •

To give real service you must add something which cannot be bought or measured with money, and that is sincerity and integrity.
—DONALD A. ADAMS

• • •

To live in the presence of great truths and eternal laws, to be led by permanent ideals–that is what keeps a man patient when the world ignores him, and calm and unspoiled when the world praises him.
—HONORÉ DE BALZAC

• • •

When faced wtih a problem, it is more productive to search for solutions rather than blame: When an archer misses the mark he turns and looks for the fault within himself. Failure to hit the bull's-eye is never the fault of the target. To improve your aim, improve yourself.
—GILBERT ARLAND

• • •

Do not lament too long when you stumble; reflect, learn, correct, and move on to success: A stumble may prevent a fall.
—THOMAS FULLER

• • •

Take time to love and imagine: I am certain of nothing but the holiness of the heart's affections and the truth of imagination.
—JOHN KEATS

• • •

A true classic, as I should like to hear it defined, is an author who has enriched the human mind, increased its treasure and caused it to advance a step; who has discovered some moral and not equivocal truth, or revealed some eternal passion in that heart where all seemed known and discovered; who has expressed his thought, observation, or invention, in no matter what form, only provided it be broad and great, refined and sensible, sane and beautiful in itself; who has spoken to all in his own peculiar style, a style which is found to be also that of the whole world, a style new without neologism, new and old, easily contemporary with all time.
—CHARLES AUGUSTIN SAINTE-BEUVE, 1850, *WHAT IS A CLASSIC?*

• • •

Reading also introduces stirring oratory to the emerging leader. You can learn from the past not only what happened but also how leaders organized the facts into a persuasive argument to convince others to agree or follow.

Imagine that you are sitting in the courtroom on July 26, 1946, at Nuremberg, Germany, listening to the closing argument of Robert H. Jackson, chief counsel for the United States in the war crimes trial of Nazi officials. Here are excerpts and the ending:

In the testimony of each defendant, at some point there was reached the familiar blank wall: Nobody knew anything about what was going on. Time after time we have heard the chorus from the dock:

"I only heard about these things here for the first time."

These men saw no evil, spoke none, and none was uttered in their presence. This claim might sound very plausible if made by one defendant. But when we put all their stories together, the impression which emerges of the Third Reich, which was to last a thousand years, is ludicrous. If we combine only the stories from the front bench, this is the ridiculous composite picture of Hitler's government that emerges. It was composed of:

Continued...

A number-two man who knew nothing of the excesses of the Gestapo which he created, and never suspected the Jewish extermination program although he was the signer of over a score of decrees which instituted the persecutions of that race;

A number-three man who was merely an innocent middleman transmitting Hitler's orders without even reading them, like a postman or delivery boy . . . A Gauleiter of Franconia whose occupation was to pour forth filthy writings about the Jews, but who had no idea that anybody would read them.

. . . . This may seem like a fantastic exaggeration, but this is what you would in actuality be obliged to conclude if you were to acquit these defendants.

They do protest too much. They deny knowing what was common knowledge.

. . . . The only question is whether the defendants' own testimony is to be credited as against the documents and other evidence of their guilt. What, then is their testimony worth?

Continued...

The fact is that the Nazi habit of economizing in the use of truth pulls the foundations out from under their own defenses. Lying has always been a highly approved Nazi technique. Hitler, in *Mein Kampf,* advocated mendacity as a policy.

. . . . Besides outright false statements and doubletalk, there are also other circumventions of truth in the nature of fantastic explanations and absurd professions. Streicher has solemnly maintained that his only thought with respect to the Jews was to resettle them on the island of Madagascar. His reason for destroying synagogues, he blandly said, was only because they were architecturally offensive.

Rosenberg was stated by his counsel to have always had in mind a "chivalrous solution" to the Jewish problem. When it was necessary to remove Schuschnigg after the Anschluss, von Ribbentrop would have had us believe that the Austrian chancellor was resting at a "villa." It was left to cross-examination to reveal that the "villa" was Buchenwald concentration camp.

Continued...

. . . It is against such a background that these defendants now ask this tribunal to say that they are not guilty of planning, executing, or conspiring to commit this long list of crimes and wrongs. They stand before the record of this trial as bloodstained Gloucester stood by the body of his slain king. He begged of the widow, as they beg of you: "Say I slew them not." And the queen replied, "Then say they were not slain. But dead they are. . . ." If you were to say of these men that they are not guilty, it would be as true to say there has been no war, there are no slain, there has been no crime.
—ROBERT H. JACKSON, CHIEF COUNSEL FOR THE UNITED STATES IN THE WAR CRIMES TRIAL OF NAZI OFFICIALS

• • •

Even the striving for equality by means of a directed economy can result only in an officially enforced inequality—an authoritarian determination of the status of each individual in the new hierarchical order. If we wish to preserve a free society, it is essential that we recognize that the desirability of a particular object is not sufficient justification for the use of coercion.
—FRIEDRICH HAYEK

Within the next generation I believe that the world's rulers will discover that infant conditioning and narco-hypnosis are more efficient, as instruments of government, than clubs and prisons, and that the lust for power can be just as completely satisfied by suggesting people into loving their servitude as by flogging and kicking them into obedience. In other words, I feel that the nightmare of *Nineteen Eighty-Four* is destined to modulate into the nightmare of a world having more resemblance to that which I imagined in *Brave New World.*
—ALDOUS HUXLEY TO GEORGE ORWELL IN OCTOBER 21, 1949 LETTER

• • •

✮ Time waits for no one. "We are here by a thread; at any time it may snap." Treasure your time and use it wisely.
—JAMES E. BROWN, SR., MD, AND *ON LEADERSHIP* EXCERPT

• • •

Keep in mind that weight gain is influenced greatly by two factors: calories ingested and calories burned. Eating gives the calories. Exercise burns the calories. For every 3,500 calories that you ingest over the amount you need to maintain your weight, you gain one pound. So if you eat more, you have to exercise more. Try walking at least five days a week. Get checked out by your physician if you have medical problems and need a custom program of exercise.
—*ON LEADERSHIP*

• • •

Iwo Jima Memorial of the raising of the U.S. Flag at Mount Surib-
achi is a symbol of sacrifice and triumph. The memorial is dedicated
to all Marines who gave their lives in the defense of the United
States since 1775.

Homework, imagination, and creativity result in this January 4, 2012 high-resolution image of Earth that was stitched together using Suomi NPP, NASA's newest Earth-watching satellite. Courtesy of NASA.

LESSONS LEARNED

- One of the greatest gifts a parent can give a child is the love of reading. The seeds of leadership often are sown at a young age.

- A lifetime of reading is important.

- Learn from the past and get inspired.

- Write down pithy quotes for later use.

- Memorize quotes from poems.

- Travel broadens one's perspective and allows you to experience cultures and appreciate what you have at home.

- Travel makes you a more interesting conversationalist.

- Observe and study to gain knowledge.

- Do not resist new adventures.

- Reflect and gain insight to gain wisdom.

- Don't let others discourage you from reading and travel.

- A leader is not a narrow-minded person.

- Eat healthful foods and exercise.

Science fiction becomes reality. Communication via satellites is a powerful means to spread liberty.

14

Putting Information Technology to Use

Doing research on the Web is like using a library assembled
piecemeal by packrats and vandalized nightly.
—ROGER EBERT

• • •

Find gadgets that you consider easy to use and reliable. There
is always someone with a love of technology willing to give
candid advice to a novice. Once hooked on the usefulness of
these devices, you never will go back to the old ways of recording
research and other documents on paper. Soon you will marvel at
the creativity of the inventors of these wonderful devices.
—*ON LEADERSHIP*

• • •

Information retrieval with modern gadgets, computers, PDAs, smartphones, and more, using wireless connections is like having a magic carpet. You can travel to the greatest libraries in the world including the National Library of Medicine.
—DJP LECTURE TO AMERICAN COLLEGE OF SURGEONS LEADERSHIP CONFERENCE 2010

• • •

The number one benefit of information technology is that it empowers people to do what they want to do. It lets people be creative. It lets people be productive. It lets people learn things they didn't think they could learn before, and so in a sense it is all about potential.
—STEVE BALLMER, MICROSOFT CEO

• • •

In the modern world of business, it is useless to be a creative, original thinker unless you can also sell what you create.
—DAVID OGILVY, ADVERTISING LEGEND

• • •

First comes information, then knowledge; but translating into wisdom is a difficult task accomplished by only a few.
—DJP, SEPTEMBER 4, 2000

• • •

I think it's fair to say that personal computers have become the most empowering tool we've ever created. They're tools of communication, they're tools of creativity, and they can be shaped by their user.
—BILL GATES, CO-FOUNDER OF MICROSOFT AND CHAIR OF THE BOARD, UNIVERSITY OF ILLINOIS URBANA-CHAMPAIGN, FEBRUARY 24, 2004

• • •

I'm also excited to see more and more schools "flip" the classroom so that passive activities like lectures are done outside of class and in-class time is used for more collaborative and personal interactions between students and teachers.
—2012 ANNUAL LETTER FROM BILL GATES, BILL & MELINDA GATES FOUNDATION

• • •

Make sure your computer information is backed up and a copy kept in a different location in event of theft, fire, flood, or other disaster. And use protective software for viruses and other "malware." Remember that even the best protection can fail with dedicated misdirected genius. In 1998, I found the CIA website name had been changed to the Central Stupidity Agency! I captured a photo of the CIA homepage before the CIA shut the site down.
—DJP

• • •

With modern technology, you can communicate around the globe in seconds.

Hackers changed name of Central Intelligence Agency to Central Stupidity Agency. DJP happened to visit site during the 20 minutes it was altered before CIA shut site down. Use anti-malware programs to try and protect your data from hackers.

Cameras are one of the many technologies that help to create gate-
ways of communication around the world.

LESSONS LEARNED

- Portable technology gadgets and information retrieval are important tools for the emerging leader.

- Having critical information but not being able to retrieve it quickly is no better than not having the information at all.

- Be creative in using cameras not only for portraits but also as storage devices for newspaper articles and documents.

- Backing up data is critical, and additional backup in another location gives important protection in the event of flood, fire, or other disaster.

- Avoid exposing digital devices to magnetic equipment to prevent data erasure.

Bullying is wrong and deters leadership. Be vigilant and demon-strate leadership by stopping bullying.

15

Bullies, An Impediment to Leadership

All cruelty springs from weakness.
—LUCIUS ANNAEUS SENECA, 4 BCE-CE 65

• • •

Courage is fire, and bullying is smoke.
—BENJAMIN DISRAELI

• • •

Whether you like it or not, history is on our side. We will bury
you.
—NIKITA KHRUSHCHEV, PREMIER, U.S.S.R.

• • •

✦ Gossip is a type of verbal terrorism. To destroy somebody's good name is to commit a kind of murder.
—RABBI JOSEPH TELUSHKIN, AUTHOR OF *WORDS THAT HURT, WORDS THAT HEAL*

• • •

If you let a bully come in your front yard, he'll be on your porch the next day and the day after that he'll rape your wife in your own bed.
—PRESIDENT LYNDON B. JOHNSON

• • •

General Secretary Gorbachev, if you seek peace, if you seek prosperity for the Soviet Union and Eastern Europe, if you seek liberalization: Come here to this gate! Mr. Gorbachev, open this gate! Mr. Gorbachev, tear down this wall!
—RONALD REAGAN SPEAKING NEARING BERLIN WALL, JUNE 12, 1987

• • •

If you let a bully intimidate you, he's going to do it again. You've got to stand up to these strong-arm tactics.
—CHARLES DJOU

• • •

Bullying can take many forms with the help of today's technology.

महात्मा गांधी   MAHATMA GANDHI

Mahatma Gandhi took a stand against British rule in India by employing non-violent civil disobedience; this paved the way to India's independence and inspired other freedom movements across the world. Gandhi proved there are peaceful ways to create change.

Never be bullied into silence. Never allow yourself to be made a victim. Accept no one's definition of your life, but define yourself.
—HARVEY S. FIRESTONE

• • •

First they ignore you, then they laugh at you, then they fight you, then you win.
—MAHATMA GANDHI

• • •

LESSONS LEARNED

- Bullies are cowards who have low self-esteem.

- Expose bullies and get help.

- Don't remain silent when observing bullies attacking someone else.

- Bullies can prevent leadership from emerging if courage is not shown.

Leaders have integrity! Their actions coincide with their words and they don't ask followers to take risks they aren't willing to take. Dr. Jim Bagian, physician, engineer, safety expert, and astronaut in June 1991 floating in Spacelab Life Sciences 1 mission (SLS-1) in Space Shuttle Columbia in orbit 185 miles above the Earth. NASA image used with permission.

Richard Anderson, MD, Chair and CEO of The Doctors Company, is another successful leader demonstrating integrity.

16

Some Leaders You May Never Have Heard of (and Some You Have)

Management is doing things right; leadership is doing the right things.
—PETER F. DRUCKER

• • •

A leader has to be brave enough to stick to his principles while being decisive, able to build a coalition based on consensus, possess the vision to guide his people and see beyond short-term obstacles, and be willing to sacrifice his own interests to serve others.
—LOUISIANA GOVERNOR BOBBY JINDAL

• • •

Leadership is about identifying where you want to go, why it is important to go, and what's in it for others—both the positive and the negative. Leaders lead by example. Leadership is personal. It is working shoulder to shoulder. You must show you are willing to get your hands dirty. You must work at least as hard as those you wish to lead. They eat first. They get sleeping quarters first. You will put yourself at risk, both professionally and physically. Leadership is service before self. Just as Ben Franklin said, "Do well by doing good."

—DR. JAMES P. BAGIAN, NASA ASTRONAUT, CORRESPONDENCE TO DJP, DECEMBER 2007, *ON LEADERSHIP*

• • •

A true leader is someone who others willingly follow.
The stronger, more independent, more thoughtful, more compe-
tent, more accomplished the followers, the better the leader must
be, and will be.
There is no true leadership in which the leader wins and the fol-
lowers lose.
—RICHARD ANDERSON, MD, CEO/CHAIR THE
DOCTORS COMPANY, *ON LEADERSHIP*

• • •

The components of leadership—be it political, professional,
civic, religious, or military—include the clarity of vision to know
where you want to go; the ability to understand and communicate the wants and needs of potential followers; the credibility to
inspire trust in those followers; the determination to persevere
when things get difficult; the skill to identify and remove obstacles along the way; and the wisdom to know when you in fact,
have arrived at your ultimate destination.
—RON FAUCHEUX, J.D., PH.D., PRESIDENT CLARUS
RESEARCH GROUP, *ON LEADERSHIP*

• • •

Essential for leadership: In a word, honesty. You can't be a good
leader and not be honest.
—LEONARD "BUD" LOMELL, RANGER WHO
DESTROYED GERMAN 155 MM CANNONS AT POINTE
DU HOC, D-DAY, JUNE 6, 1944, *ON LEADERSHIP*

• • •

Can hospitals incent staff to be more efficient by enhancing coordination and collaboration? Gain sharing engages physicians in targeted cost-reduction initiatives by rewarding them with a percentage of cost savings. . . . It has it advocates, but I agree with Donald Palmisano, a past AMA president, surgeon and attorney, who said, "First off, a physician has an ethical and fiduciary responsibility to do what's in the best interest of the patient. I think it's insulting to think that giving me an additional amount of money will make me do what I'm supposed to do."
—FLOYD D. LOOP, MD, HEART SURGEON AND CEO CLEVELAND CLINIC 1989-2004, *LEADERSHIP AND MEDICINE*

• • •

There's no such thing as a bad day when there's a doorknob on the inside of the door.
—LT. COMMANDER PAUL GALANTI, A HEROIC FRIEND AND AMERICAN NAVY PILOT, WHO SPENT ALMOST 7 YEARS IN INFAMOUS "HANOI HILTON" AS A POW

• • •

This painting depicts Ranger hero Leonard "Bud" Lomell aiming his weapon after climbing the cliffs of Point-du-Hoc in Normandy on D-Day, June 6, 1944. He destroyed the Germans' 155mm cannons. ©2006 *The Point* by Larry Selman. Reproduced with permission.

Lt. Commander Paul Galanti, U.S. Navy pilot, in the Skyhawk plane he was flying when shot down over North Vietnam. He spent almost 7 years in the infamous "Hanoi Hilton" POW camp. A wonderful and courageous American. U.S. Navy image.

They that can give up essential liberty to obtain a little temporary
safety deserve neither liberty nor safety.
—BENJAMIN FRANKLIN, NOVEMBER 11, 1755

• • •

LESSONS LEARNED

- Leadership is not limited to any one field or walk
of life.

- One can learn from the stories of current leaders as
well as past ones.

- Heroes do the extraordinary for the benefit of
others at great risk to themselves.

- Attitude is enhanced by effective communication
and can lead to survival in adverse conditions such
as a POW camp.

- In the quest for leaders, seeking out heroes is a
good starting point.

- Heroes are not limited to the field of battle.

- In the search for leaders, don't automatically eliminate those who are not perfect.

- Leaders, just as heroes, may have made mistakes in
the past. See if they learned and corrected the fault
and now warrant redemption and your support.

Fire boat response crews battle the blazing remnants of the off shore oil rig Deepwater Horizon April 21, 2010. Multiple Coast Guard helicopters, planes, and cutters responded to rescue the Deepwater Horizon's 126–person crew. (U.S. Coast Guard photo.)

GRAND ISLE, LA – A brown pelican coated in heavy oil wallows in the surf June 4, 2010. Oil form the Deepwater Horizon incident came ashore in large volumes across southern Louisiana coastal areas. Photo courtesy Win McNamee/Getty Images.

17

❦

Leadership in Crisis; the British Petroleum Gulf Oil Spill

Don't wait for federal agencies to tell you what to do. Tell them what you need.
—GOVERNOR BOBBY JINDAL IN *LEADERSHIP AND CRISIS*

• • •

"May Day, May Day. This is Deepwater Horizon. We have an uncontrollable fire." The U.S. Coast Guard log: "115 persons were recovered, some with injuries, but no casualties. Eleven persons were unaccounted for."
—*ON LEADERSHIP*, 2ND EDITION

• • •

Leadership requires prioritizing your goals above your immediate challenges. It takes knowledge, focus, discipline—but most of all courage, which cannot be bought or learned. Courage to do what is right and remain focused on your main objectives is in the heart of every leader and, I believe, the strongest characteristic that sets leaders apart from everyone else. The people of Louisiana have had tremendous courage to come back stronger from four storms in three years, and most recently the disastrous oil spill in the Gulf. The perseverance and courage of our people to always stay focused on a better tomorrow is my inspiration even through the toughest times.
—GOVERNOR BOBBY JINDAL IN *ON LEADERSHIP*, 2ND EDITION

• • •

Tomorrow doesn't mean tomorrow; it just means NOT today.
—COMMENT BY JOHN YOUNG, NOW JEFFERSON PARISH PRESIDENT, AFTER GULF OIL SPILL, REFERRING TO "FEDS," QUOTED IN GOVERNOR JINDAL'S *LEADERSHIP AND CRISIS*

• • •

Louisiana Governor Bobby Jindal, the gold standard for leadership during crisis, blazes leadership path for Louisiana with high ethics, school voucher program, and business development. DJP image

Corruption-fighter John Young elected as president of Jefferson
Parish on October 2, 2010. DJP image

The Chinese use two brush strokes to write the word "crisis." One brush stroke stands for danger; the other for opportunity. In a crisis, be aware of the danger—but recognize the opportunity.
—JOHN F. KENNEDY, SPEECH IN INDIANAPOLIS, INDIANA

• • •

Most of the important things in the world have been accomplished by people who have kept on trying when there seemed to be no hope at all.
—DALE CARNEGIE

• • •

Conflict builds character. Crisis defines it.
—STEVEN V. THULON

• • •

LESSONS LEARNED

- Listen carefully to words of wisdom from proven leaders.

- Memorize Governor Jindal's ten points for crisis leadership in his book *Leadership and Crisis*. A sampling: You must lead from the front, always. Speed is everything. There must be a sense of urgency. Listen to the locals. Keep the public informed on the details, they often know more than the Nobel Prize Laureates. Ignore the politics; focus on doing a good job.

- Never forget that courage is the fuel of leadership.

Workers in hazard suits clean oil-soaked debris along the shore
of Pensacola, FL. An important step in managing this disaster was
to get the clean-up started in addition to stopping the oil leakage.
With a disaster of this scale there is no time for hesitation.

In a crisis, leaders step forward and lead by example. Marines in
Battle of Okinawa, the bloodiest battle of WWII.
Courtesy of U.S. Library of Congress.

18

Emerging Leaders in a Time of Crisis

It is a time, in short, for a new generation of leadership—new men to cope with new problems and new opportunities.
—SENATOR JOHN F. KENNEDY, JULY 15, 1960, ON ACCEPTING THE DEMOCRATIC PARTY NOMINATION FOR THE PRESIDENCY

• • •

There cannot be a crisis today; my schedule is already full.
—HENRY KISSINGER

• • •

197

IT'S IMPORTANT FOR LEADERS TO GET THE FACTS STRAIGHT:

Crises abound. A health care bill passed in Congress with brute force by the Administration and Democratic-controlled Congress: the Patient Protection and Affordable Care Act and the Health Care and Education Reconciliation Act of 2010 (PPACA). The bill had more than 2400 pages. Most of the partisans who voted "yes" did not even read it. Remember Speaker Nancy Pelosi's words: "But we have to pass the bill so that you can find out what is in it, away from the fog of the controversy."
—DJP, *ON LEADERSHIP*, 2ND EDITION

• • •

Right now . . . if that same diabetic ends up getting their foot amputated that's 30,000 – 40,000 – 50,000 dollars immediately the surgeon is reimbursed.
—PRESIDENT BARACK OBAMA AT HEALTH TOWN HALL MEETING, NEW HAMPSHIRE, AUGUST 11, 2009, AS SEEN ON CNN

• • •

Yesterday during a town hall meeting, President Obama got his facts completely wrong. He stated that a surgeon gets paid $50,000 for a leg amputation when, in fact, Medicare pays a surgeon between $740 and $1,140 for a leg amputation. This payment also includes the evaluation of the patient on the day of the operation plus patient follow-up care that is provided for 90 days after the operation. Private insurers pay some variation of the Medicare reimbursement for this service.

Three weeks ago, the President suggested that a surgeon's decision to remove a child's tonsils is based on the desire to make a lot of money. That remark was ill-informed and dangerous, and we were dismayed by this characterization of the work surgeons do. Surgeons make decisions about recommending operations based on what's right for the patient.

—EXCERPT FROM AMERICAN COLLEGE OF SURGEONS (ACS) PRESS RELEASE, AUGUST 12, 2009, POSTED ON ACS WEBSITE

• • •

The time to guard against corruption and tyranny is before they have gotten hold of us. It is better to keep the wolf out of the fold than to trust to drawing his teeth and talons after he shall have entered.
—THOMAS JEFFERSON

• • •

The winning of freedom is not to be compared to the winning of a game—with the victory recorded forever in history. Freedom has its life in the hearts, the actions, the spirit of men and so it must be daily earned and refreshed—else like a flower cut from its life-giving roots, it will wither and die.
—DWIGHT D. EISENHOWER

• • •

The real destroyer of the liberties of any people is he who spreads among them bounties, donations and largess.
—PLUTARCH

• • •

Vietnam War Veterans Memorial. Another reminder of the cost of war. Because of the high cost in lives of brave soldiers, we must not enter war unless we are given the opportunity to win it free of political manipulation.

Symbols of our greatness in America.
Let us not dishonor them.

Experience should teach us to be most on our guard to protect liberty when the Government's purposes are beneficent. Men born to freedom are naturally alert to repel invasion of their liberty by evil-minded rulers. The greatest dangers to liberty lurk in insidious encroachment by men of zeal, well-meaning but without understanding.
—JUSTICE BRANDEIS, J., OLMSTEAD V UNITED STATES (1928) 277 US 438, 479

• • •

I believe that there are more instances of the abridgement of the freedom of the people, by gradual and silent encroachments of those in power, than by violent and sudden usurpations.
—JAMES MADISON, DEBATES IN VIRGINIA CONSTITUTIONAL CONVENTION, JUNE 6, 1788

• • •

Many in Congress have effective blockers who keep their bosses unavailable to the masses, failing to recall that the office is one of public service paid for by taxpayer monies. That causes a number of problems, not the least of which is hearing only messages inside the "bubble" and developing hubris from listening to too many sycophants.
—DJP, *ON LEADERSHIP,* 2ND EDITION

• • •

Leadership is a deep commitment to wanting to make things better for everyone. As identified in *On Leadership*, you must do your homework, work hard, and a lot of it is in one of the chapters in your book—persistence. Leadership is a lot about listening, not lecturing.
—U.S. SENATOR JOHN BARRASSO, MD, OF WYOMING

• • •

Physicians can't keep their door open to care for patients when the cost of staff salaries, office overhead, and exorbitant malpractice premiums under the broken liability system add up to more than the reimbursement for medical services paid either by the government under Medicare and Medicaid or by private insurers. This is a crisis that demonstrates the negligence and procrastination of Congress. . . . And, it also will affect the families of our brave military who are on TRICARE insurance. . . . [P]rivate contracting between patients and their physicians for medical services is needed.
—*ON LEADERSHIP,* 2ND EDITION

• • •

The power which a multiple millionaire, who may be my neighbor and perhaps my employer, has over me is very much less that that which the smallest functionaire possesses who wields the coercive power of the state, and on whose discretion it depends whether and how I am to be allowed to live or to work.
—FREDRICH VON HAYEK, *THE ROAD TO SERFDOM,* 1944

• • •

U.S. Senator John Barrasso, MD, 2010.
Photo courtesy of Donald Palmisano.

Americans know that the government is broken. According to a recent Clarus Research Poll, 80 percent agree with that conclusion. By the same overwhelming majority, Americans also agree that the government "needs a basic overhaul" and should undertake an annual "spring cleaning" to eliminate unnecessary regulations and red tape.
—PHILIP HOWARD, CHAIR OF COMMON GOOD, WRITING IN THE *WASHINGTON POST,* DECEMBER 12, 2010, *ON LEADERSHIP,* 2ND EDITION

• • •

Concentrated power is not rendered harmless by the good intentions of those who created it.
—MILTON FRIEDMAN, *CAPITALISM AND FREEDOM,* 1962

• • •

Mere passive good citizenship is not enough. Men and women must be aggressive for what is right, if government is to be saved from those who are aggressive for what is wrong.
—SENATOR ROBERT M. LAFOLLETTE, SR., 1924

• • •

We oppose a collectivist, socialistic medical system and advocate the free enterprise American system for many reasons.
National health insurance costs more.
The public always pays in the form of increased taxes.
The trusted doctor-patient relationship can only exist in a system where patients and doctors can have freedom of choice through the selection of each other. . . .
I'd like to end by stating that in closing, I bring to the attention of those who have yet to treat a sick patient, but who desire to "tinker with our medical system" the words of a son of a physician, written in the year 335 BC:
"We observe that persons of experience are actually more successful than those who possess theory without experience.
"The reason of this is that experience is acquainted with individual facts, but art with general rules, and all action and production is concerned with the individual.
"Hence, if one possesses the theory without the experience and is acquainted with the universal concept, but not with the individual facts contained under it, he will often go wrong in his treatment; for what has to be treated is the individual."
The physician's son's name? Aristotle.
—TESTIMONY OF DJP, ON BEHALF OF ORLEANS PARISH MEDICAL SOCIETY AT NATIONAL HEALTH INSURANCE HEARING MAY 20, 1976, BEFORE U.S. HOUSE OF REPRESENTATIVES, SUBCOMMITTEE ON HEALTH, COMMITTEE ON WAYS AND MEANS; REP. DAN ROSTENKOWSKI, ILLINOIS, CHAIRMAN

• • •

I was speaking to Lord Bryce just before his death, and I asked him as the best and keenest and most well-informed observer of the American people, his final judgment on them. He said: "This is true of the American people as a whole, that when they once have known the right, they have never failed at a crisis to do the right."
—REV. DR. S. PARKES CADMAN REFERRING TO JAMES BRYCE, AMBASSADOR TO THE UNITED STATES, 1907-1913 FROM *THE LAST WORDS OF DISTINGUISHED MEN AND WOMEN*, COLLECTED BY FREDERIC ROWLAND MARVIN

• • •

Politics is very much like taxes—everybody is against them, or everybody is for them, as long as they don't apply to him.
—FIORELLO H. LAGUARDIA

• • •

The capitalistic system is the oldest system in the world, and any system that has weathered the gales and chances of thousands of years must have something in it that is sound and true. We believe in the right of a man to himself, to his own property, to his own destiny, and we believe the government exists as the umpire in the game, not to come down and take the bat, but to see that the other fellows play the game according to the principles of fairness and justice.
—NICHOLAS LONGWORTH, 43RD SPEAKER OF THE U.S. HOUSE OF REPRESENTATIVES, DIED 1931

• • •

The cynic makes fun of all earnestness; he makes fun of everything and everyone who feels that something can be done. But in his heart of hearts he knows that he is a defeated man and that his cynicism is merely an expression of the fact that he has lost courage and is beaten.
—DR. GEORGE E. VINCENT

• • •

. . . It is the free market advocate that represents the best interests of the masses. It is only the free market advocate who would do away with all forms of government-granted privilege and monopoly. Ironically, it is the advocate of government action that promotes the welfare of selected favored groups at the expense of the mass of people.
—CHRISTOPHER MAYER, MISES INSTITUTE, *GOVERNMENT & BIG BUSINESS*, JULY 27, 2000

• • •

The Government's decision to spend $535 million in 2009 to Finance Solydra solar panel manufacturing is one example of heated debate regarding role of government financing of private businesses. Solydra declared bankruptcy in 2011.

The proposal is frequently made that the government ought to assume the risks that are 'too great for private industry.' This means that bureaucrats should be permitted to take risks with the taxpayers' money that no one is willing to take with his own. Such a policy would lead to evils of many different kinds. It would lead to favoritism: to the making of loans to friends, or in return for bribes. It would inevitably lead to scandals. It would lead to recriminations whenever the taxpayers' money was thrown away on enterprises that failed. It would increase the demand for socialism: for, it would properly be asked, if the government is going to bear the risks, why should it not also get the profits? What justification could there possibly be, in fact, for asking the taxpayers to take the risks while permitting private capitalists to keep the profits?
—HENRY HAZLITT, *ECONOMICS IN ONE LESSON*, 1946

• • •

Democracy extends the sphere of individual freedom; socialism restricts it. Democracy attaches all possible value to each man; socialism makes each man a mere agent, a mere number. Democracy and socialism have nothing in common but one word: equality. But notice the difference: while democracy seeks equality in liberty, socialism seeks equality in restraint and servitude.
—F.A. HAYEK, QUOTING ALEXIS DE TOCQUEVILLE (1848) IN *THE ROAD TO SERFDOM*

• • •

What our generation has forgotten is that the system of private property is the most important guaranty of freedom, not only for those who own property, but scarcely less for those who do not. It is only because the control of the means of production is divided among many people acting independently that nobody has complete power over us, that we as individuals can decide what to do with ourselves. If all the means of production were vested in a single hand, whether it be nominally that of "society" as a whole or that of a dictator, whoever exercises this control has complete power over us.
—F.A. HAYEK, *THE ROAD TO SERFDOM*

• • •

The greatest enemy to America is not another Country— It is our own Government.
—TWEET BY FORMER LOUISIANA GOVERNOR BUDDY ROEMER, MARCH 24, 2012

• • •

Former Gov. Buddy Roemer of Louisiana, a presidential
candidate, in New Orleans airport 2012.

When an Economist and former Governor/Congressman says
he's never seen Washington or Wall Street this corrupt, people
ought to listen.
— TWEET BY FORMER LOUISIANA GOVERNOR
BUDDY ROEMER, MARCH 21, 2012

• • •

The government shouldn't be picking winners and losers.
—TWEET BY FORMER LOUISIANA GOVERNOR BUDDY
ROEMER, MARCH 21, 2012

• • •

. . . Thomas Jefferson drafted the Virginia Act for Establishing
Religious Freedom in 1779, which passed in 1786, and set the
stage for the First Amendment. In it, Jefferson states: "To compel
a man to furnish contributions of money for the propagation of
opinions which he disbelieves, is sinful and tyrannical."
—QUOTED MARCH 8, 2012 IN HERITAGE'S THE
FOUNDRY'S DAILY BELL FROM A FAMILY RESEARCH
COUNCIL LETTER TO PRESIDENT OBAMA

• • •

In DJP's AMA Inaugural Address June 18, 2003, he shared the important message his heroic policeman father taught him when he considered quitting medical school, "Do your homework—have courage – and don't give up. Do that and very little in life is impossible." Here is more from that speech, Advice From the Past, Hope for the Future, *and the message is worth pondering today:*

I heeded those words. I stayed in school—and in 1963, I graduated. The rubella vaccine was still six years away. The first commercial CAT scanner—eight years away. And the discovery of moving genes from one organism to another — recombinant DNA — 10 years away.

For physicians, "doing our homework" has meant using — or pursuing — new innovations, procedures, and treatments. Keeping current with scientific literature.

Listening to our patients. And doing what is in their best interests. And because of that ethic, in 40 years as a physician, I have witnessed the miracles of organ transplants . . . vaccines . . . chemotherapy . . . long-term intravenous nutrition . . . TPN . . . and more. The eloquent Dr. Phil Berry, in the audience tonight, is living proof of one such miracle, himself a recipient of a liver transplant 17 years ago. Yesterday's science fiction is today's reality. And tomorrow will be even brighter for our young physicians.

Provided our profession is still there for them.

Because we must ask: will the next 40 years bring such life-enhancing innovation to our world — or will ominous forces subvert progress and cast us into a new Dark Age — a Dark Age of Medicine?

Continued...

With all the marvels of medical science at our fingertips, one could conclude there has never been a better time to be a physician.

Yet many physicians would disagree. As would those who once dreamed of a career in Medicine—and whose dreams have turned elsewhere.

Why would this be so?

Consider the unfunded mandates—and the tangle of regulations—that crush practices beneath an avalanche of paperwork and strangle physicians in red tape . . .

The relentless march toward centralized government control of Medicine and the price fixing, rationing, and unreasoning—and unreasonable — power of much of managed care . . .

Medicare payments locked into a flawed formula—that drives physicians from the program and ends access for vulnerable seniors . . .

Continued...

The threat to patient privacy and trust despite our best efforts to block marketeers . . .

Millions struggling without health insurance—even though most have jobs and draw a paycheck . . .

The challenge to rebuild and enhance our public health system — because the world is now a very dangerous place . . .

And a medical liability system that is fueling skyrocketing insurance premiums and system costs through lottery-style legal judgments.

Colleagues: We have to do our homework, have courage, and not give up.

And our "homework" assignment now is to assess the threats to our profession—to educate ourselves about solutions—and to prepare to fix an ailing system. And in this case, our patient is American Medicine itself.

By using the scientific method as a framework for analysis, we can make observations, gather evidence, test hypotheses, validate the findings, and prepare our argument.

This same approach can help solve the problems in law that beset the practice of Medicine. It is a powerful tool to help debunk our opponents' unfounded and ever-changing arguments.

Continued...

Our homework gives us a basis for a new health system in which everyone has insurance and everyone has choice. With defined contributions, individual ownership, and tax incentives—applicable to private or public programs—we can get coverage for all and true competition.

This allows choice among plans and selection of physicians. This puts patients—not bureaucrats—in control. Our analysis shows it can work—and it is gaining support.

—EXCERPT, AMA PRESIDENTIAL INAUGURAL ADDRESS BY DJP, JUNE 18, 2003. COMPLETE TEXT IN AUGUST 15, 2003 ISSUE OF *VITAL SPEECHES OF THE DAY*

• • •

Power tends to corrupt, and absolute power corrupts absolutely.
—LORD ACTON

• • •

All animals are equal, but some animals are more equal than
others.
—GEORGE ORWELL, *ANIMAL FARM*

• • •

[T]he sole end for which mankind are warranted, individually
or collectively, in interfering with the liberty of action of any of
their number, is self-protection. That the only purpose for which
power can be rightfully exercised over any member of a civilized
community, against his will, is to prevent harm to others. His
own good, either physical or moral, is not a sufficient warrant.
He cannot rightfully be compelled to do or forbear because it
will be better for him to do so, because it will make him happier,
because, in the opinions of others, to do so would be wise, or
even right.
—JOHN STUART MILL, *ON LIBERTY* 1869

• • •

It's important to have checks and balances in our system to ensure
no one branch of government holds too much power.

This painting depicts Benjamin Franklin, John Adams, and Thomas Jefferson reviewing a draft of the Declaration of Independence. When the tyranny of British rule became too much for the colonies, they were forced to take action.

For all tyranny does not come with tanks and jackboots. Tyranny also creeps in, like the fog, "on little cat feet." Softly, soothingly. Tyranny carries a nicely lettered sign on which it says, "This is being done for the public good." Tyranny is sly. It whispers to you and says, "You and I know what the best thing is to do. But those poor people over there are not as fortunate as you and I. They do not have the wisdom to know that what we want is really for their own good." Tyranny puts its arm around your shoulder and says, "Let's you and I save them from themselves. Let us force them to make the right choice, and later, when they are wiser, they will thank us." Tyranny says, "Let us draw up some rules to prevent the advocacy of ideas that we know are wrong. Come, let us go together and curb evil."
—TOM DILLON, SPEECH 1963, 1976 *FREEDOM MUST ADVERTISE*

• • •

A wise and frugal government, which shall restrain men from injuring one another, which shall leave them otherwise free to regulate their own pursuits of industry and improvement, and shall not take from the mouth of labor the bread it has earned. This is the sum of good government, and this is necessary to close the circle of our felicity.
—PRESIDENT THOMAS JEFFERSON FIRST INAUGURAL ADDRESS

• • •

Today was a very special day, especially with the capture of Saddam Hussein yesterday. It will be another day that will remain in my memory as long as it continues to function. The world may be a dangerous place but tonight it is a little safer, thanks to the courage and persistence of President Bush and our brave military. The potential for sunrise in Iraq and the end of darkness is within the grasp of the citizens of Iraq. Hope is a powerful stimulant for success and freedom. We are blest to live in this land of liberty called America. With time and courage and sacrifice, we may yet see liberty worldwide.

—DJP, DECEMBER 15, 2003, A BLOG UPDATE AFTER MEETING WITH PRESIDENT BUSH AND OTHERS, INCLUDING TWO IRAQI PHYSICIANS, NATIONAL SECURITY ADVISOR CONDOLEEZZA RICE, AND SENATE MAJORITY LEADER BILL FRIST, MD, IN ROOSEVELT ROOM OF WHITE HOUSE

• • •

To Dr. Donald Palmisano
With best wishes, George Bush

President Bush and Dr. Palmisano in White House Roosevelt Room December 15, 2003, the morning after Saddam Hussein was captured. Surgeon General Richard Camona, MD can be seen in background.

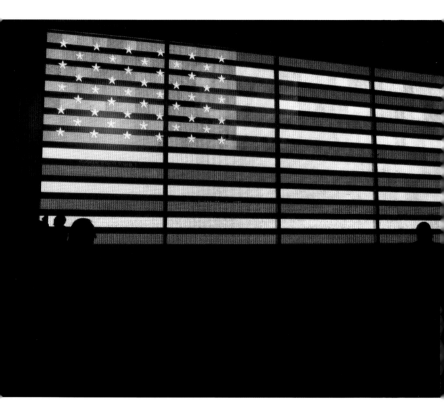

American Flag sign 2012 Times Square, New York City.

Oh, say can you see by the dawn's early light
What so proudly we hailed at the twilight's last gleaming?
Whose broad stripes and bright stars thru the perilous fight,
O'er the ramparts we watched were so gallantly streaming?
And the rocket's red glare, the bombs bursting in air,
Gave proof through the night that our flag was still there.
Oh, say does that star-spangled banner yet wave
O'er the land of the free and the home of the brave?

Oh! thus be it ever, when freemen shall stand
Between their loved home and the war's desolation!
Blest with victory and peace, may the heav'n rescued land
Praise the Power that hath made and preserved us a nation.
Then conquer we must, when our cause it is just,
And this be our motto: "In God is our trust."
And the star-spangled banner in triumph shall wave
O'er the land of the free and the home of the brave!
—THE FIRST AND LAST STANZAS OF THE STAR-SPAN-
GLED BANNER, WRITTEN BY FRANCIS SCOTT KEY IN
1814, WHILE ON BRITISH SHIP DURING BATTLE OF FORT
MCHENRY. HE WAS THERE SEEKING RELEASE OF CAP-
TURED PHYSICIAN DR. WILLIAM BEANES

• • •

Good evening. Tonight, I can report to the American people and to the world that the United States has conducted an operation that killed Osama bin Laden, the leader of al Qaeda, and a terrorist who's responsible for the murder of thousands of innocent men, women, and children. . . .
For over two decades, bin Laden has been al Qaeda's leader and symbol, and has continued to plot attacks against our country and our friends and allies. The death of bin Laden marks the most significant achievement to date in our nation's effort to defeat al Qaeda. . . .
— EXCERPT OF REMARKS BY PRESIDENT BARACK OBAMA ON THE KILLING OF OSAMA BIN LADEN, AFTER THE SUCCESSFUL RAID BY U.S. NAVY SEAL TEAM 6 IN PAKISTAN, ANNOUNCEMENT AT 11:35 PM EDT, MAY 2, 2011

• • •

Remember, if men of integrity and courage had not challenged regulations and taxes, there would have been no Declaration of Independence. Let us not forget our heritage and let us not by default desecrate the acts of Americans who died fighting throughout the world for the freedoms we enjoy today.
—DJP AT CONCLUSION OF OUTGOING SPEECH AS CHIEF OF STAFF METHODIST HOSPITAL, 1978

• • •

FREEDOM IS NOT FREE. DJP took this photo at the Korean War Memorial on Veterans Memorial Blvd. in Metairie, Louisiana, shortly after the terrorist attack of September 11, 2001. The reflection of the flags at half-mast reinforced the sadness of the times.

Editorial comment about standard used by U.S. Supreme Court to evaluate legislative acts in response to President Obama comments April 2, 2012 regarding Patient Protection and Affordable Care Act after oral arguments at U.S. Supreme Court. ©2012 Steve Kelley of the *Times-Picayune*. Reproduced with permission.

WHO HAS THE RIGHT TO REVIEW ACTS OF CONGRESS?

Ultimately, I'm confident that the Supreme Court will not take what would be an unprecedented extraordinary step of overturning a law that was passed by a strong majority of a democratically elected Congress.

—U.S. PRESIDENT BARACK OBAMA, APRIL 2, 2012, IN ROSE GARDEN PRESS CONFERENCE IN RESPONSE TO QUESTION ABOUT RECENT U.S. SUPREME COURT HEARING ON PATIENT PROTECTION AND AFFORDABLE CARE ACT

• • •

All right. I would like to have from you by noon on Thursday, that's about 48 hours from now, a letter stating what is the position of the Attorney General and the Department of Justice in regards to the recent statements by the President, stating specifically and in detail in reference to those statements what the authority is of the federal courts in this regard in terms of judicial review. That letter needs to be at least three pages, single spaced no less, and it needs to be specific. It needs to make specific reference to the President's statements and to, again, the position of the attorney general and the Department of Justice.

—U.S. FEDERAL JUDGE JERRY SMITH OF FIFTH CIRCUIT COURT OF APPEALS, APRIL 3, 2012, TO JUSTICE DEPARTMENT ATTORNEY

• • •

233

I understand the Court to have requested the views of the Department of Justice regarding judicial review of the constitutionality of Acts of Congress. The Court indicated that its inquiry was prompted by recent statements of the President. . . . The power of the courts to review the constitutionality of legislation is beyond dispute. *See generally, e.g. , Free Enterprise Fund v. Public Co. Accounting Oversight Bd. ,* 130 S. Ct. 3138 (20 10); *FCC v. Beach Communications, Inc.,* 508 U.S. 307 (1993). The Supreme Court resolved this question in *Marbury v. Madison,* 1 Cranch 137, 177-78 (1803). In that case, the Court held that "[i]t is emphatically the province and duty of the judicial department to say what the law is." *Marbury,* 1 Cranch at 177.
—ERIC H. HOLDER, JR., ATTORNEY GENERAL, APRIL 5, 2012 LETTER IN RESPONSE TO REQUEST FROM UNITED STATES COURT OF APPEALS FOR THE FIFTH CIRCUIT WHO WANTED JUSTICE DEPARTMENT POSITION ON 3 PAGES SINGLE-SPACED.

• • •

The constant aim is to divide and arrange the several offices in such a manner as that each may be a check on the other—that the private interest of every individual may be a sentinel over the public rights.
—JAMES MADISON, *THE FEDERALIST,* NO. 51 (1788)

• • •

THE ABSENT-MINDED CONSTITUTIONAL LAW PROFESSOR   www.investors.com/cartoons

Editorial comment challenging President Obama's claim April 2,
2012 about PPACA healthcare law that U.S. Supreme Court would be
taking an "unprecedented extraordinary step of overturning a law
passed by a strong majority of a democratically elected Congress."
By permission of Michael Ramirez and Creators Syndicate, Inc.

The U.S. Constitution protects our liberty and sets limits on the laws that can be implemented by Congress.

[T]he Court's power of judicial review was not confirmed until 1803, when it was invoked by Chief Justice John Marshall in Marbury v. Madison. In this decision, the Chief Justice asserted that the Supreme Court's responsibility to overturn unconstitutional legislation was a necessary consequence of its sworn duty to uphold the Constitution. That oath could not be fulfilled any other way. "It is emphatically the province of the judicial department to say what the law is," he declared.
—OFFICIAL WEBSITE OF UNITED STATES SUPREME COURT

• • •

Judicial activism is not when courts exercise their constitutional responsibility to overturn statutes that clearly violate the constitution. Rather, judicial activism is when courts ignore the constitution and instead rule on cases based on their policy preferences.
—MIKE BROWNFIELD IN HERITAGE FOUNDATION'S *THE FOUNDRY,* APRIL 6, 2012, QUOTING HERITAGE'S CULLY STIMSON

• • •

To cure, to comfort, to teach,
That is our destiny;
Not groveling before Congress,
Not fighting among ourselves for
the scraps thrown by Congress;
Not laboring under mandates
that remove us from the patient's bedside;
We are the *healers* and it is time
we found champions who will unshackle us.
—DJP, EXCERPT FROM 2008 KEYNOTE SOUTHERN
MEDICAL ASSOCIATION

• • •

LESSONS LEARNED

- It is time for a new generation of leaders.

- Americans have lost confidence in members of Congress and other elected officials.

- The U.S. Supreme Court determines if a law is constitutional.

- Voters have awakened from their apathy and want deficit spending stopped.

- True leaders tell the truth and don't demonize others falsely.

- True leaders act as guardians of trust and do not pander for voters.

A trusted patient-physician relationship is essential for quality
medicine. Science and ethics always must trump third-party
interference and coercion.

Afterword

I hope the pieces of wisdom in this book give you a clear portrait of true leadership and aid you in your journey to becoming a leader.

With true leadership in America the following can be done to enhance America's greatness. It will send a powerful example to the world and give an unequivocal message that we are a friend of liberty and a fearsome foe to our enemies:

Stand tall.
Get off bended knee.
Restore fiscal sanity to America.
Unshackle the economic engine of capitalism.
Reward hard work, creativity, and entrepreneurs.
Break the stranglehold of dependency.
Stop funding countries that help our enemies.

It is time to reward individual responsibility, stop taxing and punishing to death the pursuit of the American Dream, and let the world know we understand that a country cannot spend more money than it receives. Before we give more billions to foreign countries that disrespect us and work with those intent on doing us harm, secure our southern border! Then reassess foreign aid when we don't have to borrow the money we lend. Getting another credit card or printing money is not the solution. We need to acknowledge that and put forth a budget that is fiscally sane. Americans have had enough of the Brownian Motion that characterizes the Administration and Congress. Brownian Motion appears to be action but particles remain in the same location. Forming committee after committee is not what leaders do. Especially when no one follows the recommendations of the committees!

If you want to punish, do not attack the producers of wealth. Go after junk lawsuits, murderers, rapists, destroying mobs, and all who think they can trample the rights of Americans for their own greed and lust. Celebrate heroes, not parasites.

Yes, America, bring us true leaders, not opportunists who character assassinate those with different views. America yearns for leaders who will lead us back to greatness. And bring a plan, not just a speech. Let's see some courageous action.

Leaders have integrity, courage, decisiveness, and the ability to communicate plans carefully formulated after diligent homework. A rehash of failed economic theories is not acceptable. Stop experimental plans like the thousands of pages of the misnamed Patient Protection and Affordable Care Act (PPACA) rushed through Congress and now generating thousands of pages of regulations. Such acts are suffocating and destructive. The end does not justify the means. Liberty must be saved in America. We need fewer mandates and more opportunity.

Time is of the essence. The clock is ticking. Restore liberty and end coercion before it is too late.

Americans are brave, as evidenced by the treasure and blood we have spent since 1776 for liberty and saving other countries from tyranny. If you need a quick reminder, listen to the haunting song "Ragged Old Flag," by Johnny Cash, and reflect on our pride as Americans. Or, better yet, read the Declaration of Independence. America's greatness was not free. As I say in the epilogue of my book, *On Leadership:*

I believe Americans are disgusted . . . about the partisanship, patronage, and scandals that continue to stifle progress in Congress. The behavior in the halls and chambers of Congress also does not reflect the Declaration of Independence's conclusion: "And for the support of this Declaration, with a firm reliance on the protection of divine Providence, we mutually pledge to each other our Lives, our Fortunes and our sacred Honor.

While in the United States Air Force, I had the privilege as a surgeon to care for brave pilots returning from the war in Vietnam, and I have the greatest respect for such heroic warriors. Many of our soldiers are buried in foreign lands so that we can be free in America. But we need leadership to remain great and honor those who died for liberty. I have visited the graves of many of the fallen in Normandy, in the National Memorial Cemetery of the Pacific (at Punchbowl), and at Arlington National Cemetery. Let not their sacrifice be in vain. And to prevent the loss of more heroes, we need a consistent set of principles for engagement in wars.

Can our current leadership articulate the reason we are in multiple wars now? Terrorists targeting America? Yes, hunt them down and bring them to justice. Dictators who hurt their own people? If that is the reason we are engaging now in some lands, what about North Korea and other countries that do grievous acts to their citizens. Inconsistency reigns now. If we enter war, win quickly. Stop manipulating for political reasons. True leaders, step forward! America needs you. We must not bleed throughout foreign lands without a mission worthy of the sacrifice of lives and treasure. Review the history books about endless wars.

Leaders, we watch and wait. Don't fail us as crisis abounds. Danger is the invitation to rescue.